How to get on the property ladder

Other related titles published by How To Books

Buy to Let Property Hotspots
Where to buy property and how to let it for profit

Buy to Let Handbook
*How to invest for profit in residential property
and manage the letting yourself*

How to Make Money from Property
The expert guide to property investment

You, Property and Your Pension
*Using bricks and mortar as the safe
route to a secure retirement*

howtobooks

Please send for a free copy of the latest catalogue:

How To Books
3 Newtec Place, Magdalen Road,
Oxford OX4 1RE, United Kingdom
email: info@howtobooks.co.uk
http://www.howtobooks.co.uk

How to
get on the
property
ladder

The **first-time**
buyer's guide
to escaping
the rent trap
and owning
your own home

Ajay Ahuja BSc ACA

howtobooks

Published by How To Books Ltd
3 Newtec Place, Magdalen Road
Oxford OX4 1RE, United Kingdom
Tel: (01865) 793806 Fax: (01865) 248780
Email: info@howtobooks.co.uk
www.howtobooks.co.uk

First published 2004

British Library Cataloguing in Publication Data.
A catalogue record for this book is available from the British Library.

Produced for How To Books by Deer Park Productions, Tavistock
Typeset by PDQ Typesetting, Newcastle-under-Lyme, Staffs.
Cover design by Baseline Arts Ltd, Oxford
Printed and bound in Great Britain by Bell & Bain Ltd, Glasgow

NOTE: The material contained in this book is set out in good faith for general guidance and no liability can be accepted for loss or expense incurred as a result of relying in particular circumstances on statements made in the book. Laws and regulations are complex and liable to change, and readers should check the current position with the relevant authorities before making personal arrangements.

Contents

Part Two: Reference Section

Introduction

I bought my first home with a £500 gift from my mother in 1996 for £49,000. I can already hear you say 'it was a lot easier back then!' Ironically is was *harder* to buy a property with not a lot than it is today. The mortgage market has really opened up and now you can buy a property with nothing and get a nice cash gift of up to 25% of the property's value.

Okay, we have seen prices rise beyond belief, with the house that I originally bought being worth around £130,000, but lenders have moved with the market and more! Mortgage companies, banks and credit card companies are begging us to borrow. Every time I watch TV I see at least one advert for a loan of some sort or the other. This will not last forever. You have to take advantage of this before the lenders get their fingers burnt. I have taken advantage of it, which has amassed me a wealth of over £6 million.

I'm not saying to tie yourself up with unmanageable debt as a lot of people are doing. There are a lot of people borrowing and buying holidays, cars and unnecessary home improvements with no real plan of how to pay the lenders back. What I am saying is that you can buy a readily saleable asset – a property – with debt that is manageable from whoever is willing to lend to you. If you're a good credit risk then you'll have the pick of the bunch. If you're not a good credit risk you'll still be able to borrow at quite favourable rates.

To own a home these days you need to be cleverer than the rest. Prices are supposedly beyond the reach of the ordinary person. This is because the ordinary person is not financially aware. If they were they would realise that a property worth seven (yes seven!) times their income could be bought. They would also find out that they would probably pay less than what they are paying in rent as interest rates are at an all time low.

We all know that interest rates are at an all time low. The only way is up! Currently the interest rate will *probably* remain stable because the Euro rate is 2%, the US rate is 1.25% and Japan is 0% and we're at 4%! But you have to be prudent. Interest rates could rise to 10% within five years – no one knows which way they will go. Anyone who claims they know with certainty is a fake. If they had the capacity to know this then they could predict catastrophes such as 11 September, the Iraqi war etc.

As long as you're fed up with paying rent, want to save money, want to make money, are willing to borrow and accept a certain degree of risk then you'll be on the first rung of the property ladder before you know it. So before we get into it let me tell you about my property ladder...

My Property Ladder

I bought my first house for £49,000 in 1996 at the age of 24. I rented it out in 1997 and moved into rented accommodation for three years but continued to buy, whilst in rented accommodation, and ended up with nine rental properties by the year 2000.

I then bought my second property to live in in 2001 for £132,000 with a 5% deposit. Then I bought my third property for £240,000 with a 5% deposit in 2002 and I still live in it now. The second property is also rented out. I bought rental properties continuously during this time and I still own all the properties I have bought and they are all rented out. I am now 31 and currently looking for my next property for around £1m and I am debating whether to sell my first two properties.

I currently own over 70 investment properties and earn an income in excess of £300,000 per annum from my portfolio. I have obtained over 100 mortgages and re-mortgages in my time which certainly keeps my solicitor busy.

Why Should You Listen To Me?

I am a chartered accountant with my own practice, Accountants Direct. I know the finance industry inside out and I have first-hand experience through my property investments. I have published a number of books on property investment and I have applied this knowledge to first time buyers. I have grown my business from nothing to being worth over £6m in less than seven years. I have done this by never accepting 'no' for an answer. I have grown unorthodoxly. You could say I have 'ducked and dived' to get what I've got and I want to show you how you too can get what you want – your ultimate dream home!

Part One
How to Buy Your
First Home

1
So Why Buy a Property?

The Psychology
There is only one reason why people do not buy a property – fear.
There is only one reason why people do buy property – control.

So if you want to get on the property ladder you need to eliminate your fears and want to take control.

People's Fears
There are a number of fears that people have which are fully justified. They are not dissimilar to what business people face when appraising a potential investment. These are called risks. The difference between the ordinary person and a business person is that a business person:

a.   Identifies all the risks involved
b.   Mitigates each risk as best he or she can
c.   Considers the overall risk based on how well he or she can mitigate each individual risk
d.   Makes a decision based on the overall risk

So to get on the property ladder you need to:

a.   Identify all your fears involved in buying a property
b.   Think how you can overcome each fear involved in buying a property
c.   Consider the overall fear factor based on how well you can overcome each individual fear
d.   Decide whether you want to buy a property or not based on the overall fear factor

Fortunately for you I'm not going to ask you to think up all the fears involved in buying a property, how to overcome these fears and calculate the overall fear factor. I am going to tell you this!

Unfortunately for you I am not going to decide for you whether to buy a property or not because I am not you! However, I will present a very strong case to you and I will recommend that you buy a property – but the ultimate decision rests with you.

The Fears and How To Overcome Them

With every fear you can take what I call **countermeasures** which overcome each fear. A countermeasure is an action you take to counteract each fear. No countermeasure is fool-proof otherwise the fear would not be a fear purely by its definition as it could be fully overcome.

There will still always be an overhang of fear but it will be a lot less than the starting fear. This is what I call **residual fear**. The residual fear is therefore still present even after the countermeasure and thus is a real fear. You can take further countermeasures to reduce this residual fear but it depends on how far you want to go.

There will always be residual fear however. An example of residual fear that cannot be eliminated is the destruction of your house if there was a war. No insurance company will take on this risk. The only way you could mitigate this risk would be to build a bomb-proof shell around your house – but this would be impractical and probably cost more than your house itself!

The fears, countermeasures and residual fears in buying a property are:

	Fear	Countermeasure	Residual fear	Further countermeasures
1	Losing your job and can't pay the mortgage.	Buy a property that can be easily let out and the rent covers the mortgage payment comfortably.	The tenant does not pay the rent.	Take out landlord insurance that covers you for loss of rent due to tenant default.
2	Interest rate rises beyond affordability.	Fix the interest rate for a fixed period of time.	The interest rate rises beyond affordability after the fixed period of time.	Fix the interest rate for the whole term of the mortgage.
3	Get caught in negative equity trap.	Don't sell the property and realise your loss. Rent it out. Wait for the recovery and then sell.	It never recovers and you have to sell.	Take out a smaller unsecured loan to cover the different between the selling price and mortgage balance.

4	Have to move out of the area due to a change of job.	Buy a property that can be easily let out and the rent covers the mortgage payment comfortably.	The tenant does not pay the rent.	Take out landlord insurance that covers you for loss of rent due to tenant default.
5	Major repair becomes due and can't afford to carry out works.	Take out a thorough and comprehensive buildings and contents insurance.	The policy doesn't capture every eventuality,	Take out specific policies for specific items, i.e. British Gas offer full insurance on your boiler from £8 per month.
6	Buying a property you can't sell.	Avoid difficult to sell properties such as studio flats, ex local authority flats, flats above shops, non-standard construction properties or any property that is difficult to get a mortgage on.	Still can't sell it!	Buy a property near a city train station or major road junction.
7	Financially linking yourself with a partner and becoming liable for their share.	Create a document that transfers full ownership to you if your partner defaults.	Still can't afford to pay their share.	Buy a saleable property (i.e. an easily mortgageable one) and sell it! Or rent it out.
8	Can't pay the mortgage as it falls due, due to the irregularity of your income.	Get a flexible mortgage where you can overpay on the mortgage and take payment holidays.	Still can't afford to pay the mortgage.	Get an overdraft facility or pay the mortgage with your credit card cheque book and pay back when able to do so.

Real Life Examples

Case	Fear	Countermeasures
Robert	Robert was uncertain about his job as there had been a few redundancies in the past. He was worried about whether he would be able to afford the mortgage repayments if he lost his job.	I recommended him to buy a property in the easily lettable areas for no more than £80,000. This meant that his mortgage costs would be no more than £267 per month at a five-year fixed rate. If he were to rent the property out he would get £400 per month after tenant insurance premiums. So in the eventuality he did lose his job he could cover the mortgage by letting the property out. There is also a profit margin there so he could hand the property over to a letting agent and let them deal with it and still maintain the mortgage payments. Robert could then focus on finding another job!

Case	Fear	Countermeasures
Julie	Julie was worried that even though she could afford the mortgage now at current rates, interest rates could rise beyond affordability in the next three years.	I recommended that she fix the interest rate for five years so that the mortgage payment would be the same for the whole five years. I also recommended she make overpayments to the mortgage thus reducing her overall balance so that the likely interest cost after the five years would be lower than if she did not make these overpayments.
Alex	Alex was worried about buying a property that he could not sell in two years for more money than he bought it for.	I recommended that Alex bought a property that needed work in a lettable area, non-ex local authority and of standard construction for no more than £75,000. This way he would add value to the property when the work was done. When it comes to selling the property it would be likely that he would at least get his money back if not more. In the eventuality that it was worth less than what he had paid then I advised that he could rent it out for £450 with a mortgage payment of only £250, giving him a good excess of rent over mortgage payments thus allowing for voids, agent fees and repairs.

Overall Fear

To calculate your overall fear is to gather all the residual fears that remain. To do this you:

a. Decide which fears listed above, 1 to 8, are fears that you actually have
b. Decide what countermeasures you are willing to take for each fear
c. Calculate the residual fear for each fear applicable

So for example if you had the following fears and were willing to take the following countermeasures then your overall fear is all the contents of the residual fear column.

Fear	Countermeasures willing to take	Residual fear
1 Losing your job and can't pay the mortgage.	Buy a property that can be easily let out and for which the rent will cover the mortgage payment comfortably.	The tenant does not pay the rent.
3 You get caught in the negative equity trap.	Don't sell the property and realise your loss. Rent it out. Wait for the recovery and then sell.	It never recovers and you have to sell.
4 You have to move out of the area due to change of job.	Buy a property that can be easily let out and for which the rent will cover the mortgage payment comfortably.	The tenant does not pay the rent.

| 6 | Buying a property you can't sell. | None. | | Buying a property you can't sell. |
| 8 | You can't pay the mortgage as it falls due, due to the irregularity of your income. | None. | | You can't pay the mortgage as it falls due, due to the irregularity of your income. |

So the overall fear is that if you needed to let the property out the tenant wouldn't pay; the property will fall in value below what you paid for it; the property becomes unsaleable and you won't be able to pay the mortgage on time.

If you are happy with this overall fear then you will buy a property. If you are not then you won't buy a property. If you are not happy with the overall fear then I suggest you take more countermeasures so that your overall fear is reduced to a level that you are happy with.

But to take on an overall fear there must be some benefits! This leads on nicely to the benefits of owning a property.

The Benefits of Owning A Property

People take on the 'pain' or overall fear of owning a property because of the 'pleasure' or benefits of owning a property. It's the simple pain-pleasure principle. If the pleasure can outweigh the pain then we take action.

We've identified the pain element – so what's the pleasure? Here are some of the benefits of owning a property that override the overall fear of owning a property.

	Benefits	Description
1	Its cheaper!	Mortgage payments are invariably cheaper than rent unless you rent at the very top end of the market. The mortgage market is very competitive at the moment and theoretically you can reduce your living costs by up to 70%!
		Tenants pay a premium to rent a house because the landlord is taking full risk on owning the property. I am a landlord and I am very happy to take this premium as I consider the risk of owning a property low compared to the reward I receive as rent.
		If you can get your overall fear of owning a property to a manageable level then the cost savings benefit alone makes it worthwhile.

	Benefits	Description
2	Creates deposit for the next home	The equity you build up in the property can be used to buy your next property. If you buy a flat for £50,000 with a 100% mortgage and the price rises to £80,000 in five years then you have amassed £30,000 in equity. You can then use this £30,000 equity as a deposit and by doing this it opens up the mortgage market. You will then be able to go to a higher income multiple lender. Also, if your income has increased by 20% over the five years then you could buy a house worth £110,000. This could mean moving from a one-bed flat to a two-bed semi in a better area. If you didn't have the equity then you would have to buy this same house on a 100% mortgage. This would mean that your income would have needed to double for you to afford this same house. You then have to estimate how likely that is. So buying you first house makes it easier to get a better property further down the line.
3	You're not at the mercy of your landlord	If you rent a property then it is not your property! Property law dictates that a landlord can get possession of a property by giving the tenant two months' notice. The landlord does not need to give a reason why. It is their right to seek possession as the landlord owns the property. So you may get very settled in your landlord's property, make friends and really get accustomed to the area. But lo and behold the landlord returns from their trip around the world and wants their property back! You have no grounds for defence – you have to get out! By owning your own property you have full peace of mind that you can stay there as long as you want. There will be no landlord ready and waiting to take back your property. The only way you can lose your property is if you do not keep up with your mortgage payments or the house falls under a compulsory purchase order. If you can't keep up with your mortgage payments then you definitely can't keep up with your rent so you'd get thrown out anyway. Compulsory purchase orders are very rare and are hard to predict. Owning your own property gives you independence and control over how you live your life.
4	You can add value to your living space	Paying rent is money down the drain. We all know that. But improvements to your own living space in rented accommodation are even more money down the drain! If you're fed up with the kitchen or bathroom of your property and replace either or both then you will never recoup the cost of this. The only person who will, will be your landlord! You will only add value to a property that is not yours. If you own your own property and make selective improvements then the full cost or more can be recouped when you come to sell the property. This cost will not only make living at your property more enjoyable but will add real money to the eventual selling price of the property.

I have to be honest. I decided to own my first property based on the four reasons above rather than any of the eight fears listed above. It just seemed to make sense. With hindsight I should have considered the eight fears as I would have chosen a different property than the one that I chose – and made a lot more money. But I cannot complain. Even though my property hasn't trebled or quadrupled in value, as it would have done if I had followed my own advice, I still own my first property, which is rented out and that earns me a steady income now.

I hope you can see from the above that not owning a property is worse than owning a property. Obviously owning an asset, like property, carries a certain degree of risk and responsibility but the pleasure clearly outweighs the pain.

I hope I have convinced you into buying your first property. Now to the next part – actually buying one!

Identify Your Status Ranking

What is Status Ranking?

Status ranking is a measure of how financially sound you are. It is a ranking of your financial status, which you give yourself, based on the facts and habits you have with money. It incorporates how you save and spend your money in the present and in the *previous six years*.

Money fits in to two broad categories:

1. Savings
2. Income

Savings

Savings is basically a lump sum of money that you have put away to spend on something that does not form part of your day-to-day spendings. For example a car, a holiday or even...a *house*! The existence (or non-existence!) of savings and the amounts can give you a fair indication of how you handle your money.

Income

Income is a sum of money that comes into the pot on a fairly regular basis, usually weekly or monthly, i.e. salary, and is spent on day-to-day living expenses. For example food, clothes or even...a *mortgage*! How you spend this income and the amounts can give you a fair indication of how you handle your money.

Credit History

Whenever you require money from someone, like a bank, they need to have an indication of how you handle your money. There are credit reference agencies out there that monitor whether you handle money well or badly.

Virtually everyone has a credit history. The only people that don't are people who have never obtained credit i.e. borrowed money or had a credit card. These people are usually school leavers or students and their credit history will show nil activity. For them I would suggest getting a credit card or contract phone to kick start your credit file. For the rest of us these agencies record how much credit we obtain and whether we kept to our side of the bargain. In other words have we paid them back and on time!

This information is kept for six years and monitors:

- mortgage repayments
- loan repayments
- credit card repayments
- store card repayments
- household bill repayments
- County Court Judgements (CCJs).

So to identify your status ranking you need to think about these three key factors:

1. Whether you save money and how much.
2. How much you earn, how you spend money and the amounts spent.
3. Your credit history.

The Status Ranking Table

Based on the factors above, how you save and spend your money in the present and in the previous six years, you can come up with a table that ranks your status.

Status ranking	Name	Credit history	Savings	Income	Description
1	Prime lazy coward	Good	Enough for a deposit	Enough to afford a mortgage	The highest rank but you should be ashamed of yourself! There is no real reason why you're not on the property ladder already unless you're either scared, lazy or both! There is nothing to stop you going out now and buying yourself a property and taking that first step to owning your ultimate dream home.

Status ranking	Name	Credit history	Savings	Income	Description
2	Prime saver	Good	Enough for a deposit	Not enough to afford a mortgage	Ok, you can save money, and it seems like you are spending less than you earn. It could be that you're looking at the wrong types of property, looking in the wrong areas and/or not choosing the right financial products.
3	Prime hi-flyer	Good	Not enough for a deposit	Enough to afford a mortgage	You're on a good whack but have problems saving any of it! You seem to be spending as much or more than you earn. Ironically, you will have a good income but you'll have credit card balances and loans to fund your overspending.
4	Adverse lazy coward	Bad	Enough for a deposit	Enough to afford a mortgage	Again you are either lazy, scared or both. There are many financial products out there that cater for financially sound applicants with previous bad credit history.
5	Adverse saver	Bad	Enough for a deposit	Not enough to afford a mortgage	Ok, you can save money, and it seems like you are spending less than you earn. It could be that you're looking at the wrong types of property, looking in the wrong areas and/or not choosing the right financial products.
6	Prime struggler	Good	Not enough for a deposit	Not enough to afford a mortgage	You spend all or more than you earn and every property in your area is way too expensive – life seems a constant struggle! You're looking at the wrong types of property, looking in the wrong areas and/or not choosing the right financial products.
7	Adverse hi-flyer	Bad	Not enough for a deposit	Enough to afford a mortgage	You're on a good whack but have problems saving any of it! You seem to be spending as much or more than you earn. Ironically, you will have a good income but you'll have credit card balances and loans to fund your over-spending. Knowledge of financial products is limited.
8	Adverse struggler	Bad	Not enough for a deposit	Not enough to afford a mortgage	The lowest rank and you should be ashamed of yourself! You've got no money and you've defaulted in the past. However, you too can still get on the property ladder. The choice may be limited and there is above average risk but it is still possible.

Ranking Order Justifications

The rankings 1 and 8 are absolutes. That is, status ranking 1 is superior to all the others and status ranking 8 is inferior to all the others. Status rankings 2–7 are subjective. I have ranked them according to my own experience with dealing with my clients and criteria set out by mortgage lenders.

Example People with Status Rankings 1–8

Status Ranking 1 – Prime Lazy Coward

Mandy is aged 31, lives in Birmingham and earns £28,000 per year. She saves £300 per month and has £8,000 in savings. She has good credit history and pays rent of £450 per month.

Mandy takes home £1,750 per month. After rent and other living expenses she treats herself to a modest trip to the high street, every fortnight or so. She shops in the sales and always clears her credit card balance. She bought her car for cash to get the best discount on the car. She is careful when she goes out and budgets her monthly expenditure with every major expense fully thought out and justified. She is disciplined to save £300 per month. She has no overdraft facility or personal loans.

Is this you? Do you earn a good wage? Do you have savings over £5,000? Do you budget your forthcoming expenditure and save consistently? Think – do you pay rent that is in excess of your co-worker's mortgage? Then do not get left behind! Get out to your local estate agents now and join their mailing lists – pronto!

Two-bed flats in Birmingham typically go for around £70,000. From reading this book you'll find out that she can put a 10% deposit down, £7,000, and get a residential mortgage for £63,000. The monthly cost at current rates equate to £236. So Mandy not only gets on to the property ladder but saves herself £214 per month. So based on this example Mandy is either lazy and/or scared. If I was being harsher I would say stupid!

Status Ranking 2 – Prime Saver

David is aged 25, lives in London and earns £25,000 per year. He saves £250 per month and has £6,000 in savings. He has good credit history and pays rent of £350 per month sharing a flat with two colleagues.

David is a young professional. He has a good job working as a trainee in an accountancy firm. He's frustrated that even though he earns okay money, saves well and has good credit history, he still can't even afford a grotty studio flat near his place of work.

Are you frustrated at the current property prices? Can't understand why you can't get on to the property ladder even though you have a half decent job?

Studio flats in London typically go for around £100,000. He can put a 10% deposit down on a 50% shared ownership flat, £5,000, and get a residential mortgage for £45,000. The monthly cost at current rates equate to £169. He will pay a subsidised rent of £109 per month. Total monthly cost £278. So David not only gets on to the property ladder but saves himself £72 per month. He can also buy the other 50% share when he earns more in the future.

Status Ranking 3 – Prime Hi-Flyer
Zak is aged 30, lives in London and earns £55,000 per year. He saves £nil per month and has £1,000 in savings. He has good credit history and pays rent of £1,000 per month sharing a flat with a friend in Knightsbridge.

Zak is an investment banker. He has a high profile job and he socialises with friends and colleagues who earn an income equal to or greater than his own. If there is a party – he's there! If his group plan a high spending holiday – he's there! He spends what he earns and more. He has several credit cards, several loans and several girlfriends!

Do you lead a life of excess? Is this life of excess proving to be not much fun now? Are your friends acquiring more than you?

One-bed flats in central London typically go for around £180,000. From reading this book you'll find out that he can put no deposit down and get a 100% residential mortgage for £180,000. The monthly cost at current rates equate to £675. So Zak not only gets on to the property ladder but saves himself £325 per month.

Status Ranking 4 – Adverse Lazy Coward
Sarah – same as Mandy above but got into a bit of financial trouble.

Sarah split from her boyfriend three years ago. Joint name credit cards got settled late and there were defaults on their joint mortgage and the telephone bill didn't get paid. Now she has put this all behind her, settled all outstanding debts, and now has savings and spends less than her income.

Is this you? Had some difficulties but back on track? Do you earn a good wage? Do you have savings over £5,000? Do you budget your forthcoming expenditure and save consistently?

Sarah could buy the same flat as Mandy but pay a higher interest rate. Her monthly cost would be £341. Sarah gets on the ladder, despite her history, and saves £109!

Status Ranking 5 – Adverse Saver
Gavin – same as David above but got into a bit of financial trouble.

Gavin bought a car on HP four years ago. He was young, 21, and wanted a flash car to impress his friends but more importantly – the ladies! After six months he wrote the car off – but not the debt! He chose not to pay the debt but the finance company took him to court to enforce the debt and won. He now pays £200 per month to clear the debt but has a county court judgement (CCJ) registered against him.

Do you think that you are unable to get a mortgage because of your CCJs? Are you earning good money now? Have you learnt from your past mistakes?

Gavin could get the same flat as David but again pay a higher interest rate. His monthly cost would be £244. Gavin still gets on the ladder, despite his history, and saves £106 per month!

Status Ranking 6 – Prime Struggler
Abdul is aged 24, lives in Rochester and earns £22,000 per year. He saves £nil per month and has £500 in savings. He has good credit history and pays rent of £150 per month to his parents as he lives at home.

Abdul spends all his cash, saves nothing and lives in an area where he is priced out. He lives at home, where it is cheap, but is concerned that he cannot live at his parents' house forever and he might miss the boat when it comes to getting on to the property ladder. He feels snookered.

Is this you? Are you priced out? Have no savings? Comfortable where you are but concerned?

Abdul could buy a studio flat near where he lives now, in an area like Chatham, for £52,000 on a 100% mortgage. His monthly cost will be £195 per month. This is in excess of his current living costs but he is on the property ladder – come on, you can't have everything!

Status Ranking 7 – Adverse Hi-Flyer
John – same as Zak but has got into a bit of financial trouble.

John, trying to keep up with his friends, ran up an unmanageable credit card debt a year ago. He settled out of court and now pays £100 per month and the interest charge was frozen. No CCJ was registered but a default was.

Is your credit history possibly not as bad as you think? On a top wage now? Ready to start again?

John could get the same flat as Zak but pay a higher interest rate. His monthly cost would be £975. John gets on the ladder, despite his history, and saves £25 per month.

Status Ranking 8 – Adverse Struggler
Natalie – same as Abdul but has got into a bit of financial trouble.

Natalie went through a bad period in her life and ran up significant store and credit card debts. She got taken to court and has three CCJs registered against her. She has settled one of them and is paying regularly on the other two. She needs to live in Rochester, which is more than she can afford, and she has been self-employed for only two years with no accounts.

Is this you? Do you have CCJs? Are you self-employed less than three years with no accounts? Do you need to live in the area?

From reading this book you'll find out that Natalie could get a self-certified unsecured loan to raise a 10% deposit on an £80,000 adverse credit mortgage to buy a studio in Rochester. The total monthly cost including the loan repayment would be £690. It is a lot more than £150 per month at home but she can afford it and more importantly, she gets on the property ladder.

So Which Status Ranking Are You?

Hopefully, from the above table and examples, you would have identified what status ranking you are. You have to be honest with yourself. Do not rank yourself what you want to be. Rank yourself who you actually are! If you can't save, have no deposit and have bad credit then there is no point applying for a mortgage that is out of your reach. You will be wasting a lot of people's time, and most importantly – *yours*!

Looking at the table it's not difficult to realise that the aim is to rise up the status ranking table. Rising up the table increases your 'buying power' thus increasing the range of properties available to you. Ways to increase your status ranking are dealt with in Chapter 5 but the next chapter deals with buying power.

3
Calculating Your
Buying Power

What is Buying Power?

Buying power is your ability to actually buy a property. It is as simple as that. So what enables you to actually buy a property? Buying power follows this simple equation:

BUYING POWER = (deposit you actually have) + (mortgage you're able to get)

Each part of the equation is dependent on the other. The mortgage you are able to get is dependent on the deposit level you have. If the mortgage requires a deposit level but you do not have a deposit then it doesn't matter how much you earn – your buying power is *zero*!

So let's look at this simple example:

Katy is at status ranking 4. She earns £30,000 per year, she has £8,000 in the bank and has bad credit. She applies to an adverse credit lender who offer her a standard 3.5 times her salary as borrowings. Her buying power equates to:

(£8,000) + (3.5 × £30,000 = £105,000) = £113,000
(deposit you actually have) + (mortgage you're able to get) = BUYING POWER

So Katy can buy a property up to a value of £113,000. Katy will be very happy if she wants to buy a property for £80,000 as she can clearly afford this. What happens if she wants to buy a property for £150,000?

Obviously she needs to increase her buying power. So how does she do this? Find out below.

Increasing Buying Power

Can I remind you of what I said in the earlier chapter about status rankings:

'So to identify your status ranking you need to think about these three key factors:

1. *Whether you save money and how much.*
2. *How much money you earn, how you spend money and the amounts spent.*
3. *Your credit history.'*

To increase buying power you need to think about these three key factors:

1. Whether you save money and how much.
2. How much you earn, how you spend money and the amounts spent.
3. Your credit history.

Spot the similarity?

The factors involved in rising up the status ranking are the same as the factors involved in increasing your buying power. To rise up the status ranking you automatically increase your buying power. Let me explain why, looking at each factor in turn.

Whether You Save Money and How Much

Let me remind you of the buying power equation:

BUYING POWER = (deposit you actually have) + (mortgage you're able to get)

If you save money then you can only increase the deposit you actually have. The more money you have to put down the greater your buying power is.

Let me remind you of the status ranking:

If you have 'enough for a deposit' then you are ranked, assuming all other factors equal, higher than someone who does 'not have enough for a deposit'. So if you save and get to a level that takes you from not having enough to having enough then your ranking rises.

So the key point is to *save*! Saving also has a doubling effect. Due to the way mortgage companies work, the more deposit you have the more you can:

1. Increase the number of lenders wishing to lend to you thus increasing your choice of lender.

2. Increase the income multiples offered to you thus increasing your buying power.

3. Reduce the amount of mortgage relative to the property price thus lowering the risk to lender and resulting in a lower interest rate.

So if Katy saved further and had £12,000 to put down she could go to a different lender offering her four times her salary. Thus her buying power is:

£12,000 + (4 × £30,000) = £132,000.

So Katy has increased her buying power from £113,000 to £132,000 – that's an increase of £19,000 by simply having £4,000 more to put down as a deposit (£12,000 − £8,000 = £4,000).

Tips on how to save are detailed in Chapter 5 – Increasing your Buying Power by Increasing Your Status Ranking.

How Much You Earn, How You Spend Money and the Amounts Spent

Let me remind you of the buying power equation:

BUYING POWER = (deposit you actually have) + (mortgage you're able to get)

If you earn more money then you can only increase the mortgage you're able to get. The more money you earn the higher your buying power is. So in our above example, if Katy increased her earnings to £35,000 then she could get, assuming all other factors equal, a mortgage for 3.5 x £35,000 = £122,500. This would mean her buying power increases from £113,000 to £130,500 – an increase of £17,500.

I can hear what you're saying – how on earth do I increase my earnings? It depends on you! Tips on how to increase your earnings are detailed in Chapter 5 – Increasing your Buying Power by Increasing Your Status Ranking.

Your Credit History

Your credit history has a direct effect on your status ranking and an indirect effect on your buying power.

If your credit history is improved then, all things being equal, it increases your status ranking. This will only increase your buying power due to the wider range of financial products available to you.

Your credit history affects the total amount you can borrow and, if your credit history is good, it reduces the amount you need to put down as a deposit. For example if you have bad credit, no deposit and can only get a 90% mortgage then you can't buy anything hence buying power = 0. If you improve your credit then you can get a 100% mortgage hence your buying power = something, and you can buy a property for no money down.

Tips on how to improve your credit history are in Chapter 5 – Increasing your Buying Power by Increasing Your Status Ranking.

4
Understanding
the Mortgage Game

The Importance of Understanding the Mortgage Game

If you want to buy a property, usually you have to buy it with a combination of your money (being your deposit) and the bank's money (being the mortgage). In my experience the combination of your money to the bank's is 10:90. That is to say the bank contributes a substantial amount, being 90% of the purchase price and you contribute 10%.

So guess how important the purchase is to the bank compared to you? About nine times more important! That is why understanding how they operate is very important. If they don't want to lend to you then you can forget about owning any property unless you have enough to buy the property for cash. Buying power is highly dependent on being able to obtain a mortgage. Chapter 5, 'Increasing Your Buying Power by Increasing Your Status Ranking', deals with preparing yourself for getting a mortgage.

Once you understand the mortgage game you can use this knowledge to exploit them. I use the term 'game' because it is a game – you have to jump through *their* hoops. We cannot eliminate these hoops but we can certainly lower these hoops so they're easier to jump through. Chapter 6, Increasing Your Buying Power *Without* Increasing Your Status Ranking, deals with this very topic.

What Mortgage Companies Look For

In a nutshell, what mortgage companies look for is – are you a good bet? How do they establish this? I think you might remember this from previous chapters:

1. Whether you save money and how much.
2. How much you earn, how you spend money and the amounts spent.
3. Your credit history.

So mortgage companies need to establish the above. How do they do this? Find out how they do this and, more importantly, how to exploit this below.

Whether You Save Money and How Much

This, apparently, is easy for mortgage lenders to establish. Most will want to know that you have the ability to save money for a rainy day – a typical rainy day being that you lose your job and can't afford the mortgage. A person who saves will have money put aside for this rainy day. So how do they know if you save money? If you have a cash deposit to put down to buy a property then the mortgage lenders think you can save money – regardless of where that cash deposit came from!

I say most lenders, some do not. These are called 100% mortgages. That is to say they lend 100% of the purchase price. Some lenders even lend in excess of 100%. There are a few specialist lenders out there that offer up to 115% of the purchase price. In effect – they pay you to buy a property!

Generally though you need at least a 5% deposit. The more deposit you have the better range of interest rates you get. When you have a deposit of 25% then you have the choice of virtually the whole market. So the more you save now to put down the less you will pay in interest. Let me show you this example of how much you could save.

Emily wants to buy a house for £100,000. She has £10,000 to put down. She finds out that she can get a mortgage for 5% interest rate for 25 years if she puts a 10% deposit down.

She then passes a garage selling a beautiful BMW for £5,000, and guess what, she just can't resist it and pays for it out of her deposit.

She then finds out that if she puts only a 5% deposit she has to pay 5.5% interest rate. So lets look at the costs:

If she didn't buy the BMW:

$$£90,000 \times 5\% \times 25 \text{ years} = £112,500 \text{ total cost of interest}$$

If she did buy the BMW:

$$\pounds95,000 \times 5.5\% \times 25 \text{ years} = \pounds130,625 \text{ total cost of interest}$$
(Interest only mortgages)

So the difference in cost is £18,125. So in effect the BMW, worth £5,000, cost £18,125! That's bad value. If she spent the whole £10,000 on a better BMW the difference would have been even worse. She would have lost around £30,000.

Hopefully you can see the power of having a deposit. If you have any cash put away – preserve it, it's precious.

How Much You Earn, How You Spend Money and the Amounts Spent

What mortgage lenders need to know are:

1. Can you afford to pay back what they've lent you including the interest?
2. Can you do this for the duration of the loan?

It's called serviceability. They will judge this on:

1. How much you earn.
2. How and what you spend your money on.
3. How long you've been in your current employment or self-employment.

These factors seem reasonable. Would you lend £1,000 to your friend who has been unemployed for three years, spent the majority of his dole money on cannabis and just started a job in McDonalds earning £5 per hour? I know I wouldn't! So it is not unreasonable to expect a mortgage lender to know a little bit about how we earn and spend our money.

The first question they're going to ask is how much do you earn? Lenders do not like to lend more than what you can afford. They estimate that up to 30% of your salary can be used to pay a mortgage. It is likely that the other 70% will be taken up on other living expenses such as travel, household bills, food and clothing. Based on this they will lend around three to four times your salary. This multiple, three or four times your salary, was set a number of years ago when interest rates were around 8%. Due to low interest rates you will find out that you will be able to afford up to five times your salary and there are certain lenders out there that know this and offer mortgages based on this.

So once they know how much you earn they need to know how you spend it. Lenders do not automatically lend three to four times your salary. They need to know that there is that actual surplus of around 30%. Take, for example, Ken, who earns £2,000 per month. If he's got a car on HP, insurance costs, various loans, credit card debts and travelling expenses totalling £1,900 then they will not lend to him. This is because in his current state he can't even afford to pay rent – let alone a mortgage! Lenders usually ask for an affordability statement. This is a statement where you detail what money comes in and what money goes out.

After finding out how much you earn and how you spend it they need to know if the money is still going to keep flowing in! They base this on length of employment. The usual time periods are:

1. One year for employment
2. Three years for self-employment

How you prove this to the lender is wage slips for the last three months for the employed or three years' accounts certified by a qualified accountant for the self-employed.

What you'll find out in Chapter 6, Increasing Your Buying Power *Without* Increasing Your Status Ranking, is that there are lenders that are willing to be a little bit flexible in making these judgements.

Your Credit History

You may be a good bet now – but were you in the past? They will need to establish your creditworthiness in the past and present so they can predict your creditworthiness in the future.

There are two main credit reference agencies that all lenders consult before they make any lending decision, Experian and Equifax. They record a number of details about you based on your current and previous addresses in the last three years, namely:

1. **Electoral Roll** – whether you are on the electoral roll. Some lenders require you to be on the electoral role before they can lend.

2. **County Court Judgments (CCJs)** – these arise when you have been taken to court by a debtor to enforce payment of a debt and the debtor won the case. The court holds this information for six years from the date of the judgment. They also record if you subsequently paid the judgement.

3. **Individual Voluntary Arrangements (IVAs)** – this is where you have become bankrupt and unable to pay your debts. Once you have been made bankrupt and the debts have been settled then you become a discharged bankrupt. Only once you have been discharged can you have any hope of obtaining credit again. You are automatically discharged after six years.

4. **Credit accounts** – these are all your loan accounts that have been active in the last six years and whether you have ever defaulted on them. Typical accounts are your mortgage account, credit and store card accounts and personal loans.

5. **Repossessions** – details of any house repossessions that have ever occurred.

6. **Previous searches** – these are previous credit searches by other lenders that you have made a credit application with.

7. **Gone Away Information Network (GAIN)** – this is where you have moved home and not forwarded on the new address and not satisfied the debt.

8. **Credit Industry Fraud Avoidance System (CIFAS)** – this is where the lender suspects fraud and just flags it up. You cannot be refused credit based on a suspicion.

Your credit file dictates the mortgage you can get. The key factors are CCJs or defaults. If you have any CCJs or defaults (points 2 and 4 above) you will be restricted to adverse credit lenders who charge higher arrangement fees and interest rates. If you have an IVA, repossession or GAIN on your file it is unlikely you will get a buy-to-let mortgage but you will be able to get a residential mortgage depending on when you had debt problems. It is worth noting that the buy-to-let mortgage market is further developing and a suitable product may come on to the market soon.

There is one key thing you should remember when filling out your form – do not lie! If lenders find out they will demand repayment in full and they could inform the police of fraud – the charge being obtaining finance by deception. The credit reference agencies are becoming more and more sophisticated. They log every bit of information you put on every credit application and if you submit an application that was slightly different from a previous application they will flag it up.

There is a list of adverse lenders in the reference chapter.

The Main Reasons Why People Are Declined

1. When you apply for a mortgage or any type of credit, a lender will look into your credit history by contacting Experian or Equifax, the credit reference agencies. If they've found out that you have failed to repay your debts in the past, it will affect your chances of getting a mortgage, loan or credit card. Late payments, County Court Judgments (CCJs) and Repossession Orders can all lead to refusal.

2. Lenders will also take into consideration the debts you have already and compare this to your income. If they believe you have insufficient funds to repay the loan, again they will turn down your application.

3. If you have been 'shopping around' for credit, there will be searches registered on your credit file. In some cases this will be sufficient reason for lenders to refuse you any further credit even though you have no intention of taking the credit applied for.

The Different Types of Mortgages

There are three core elements to a residential mortgage. They are:

1. Whether it is an interest only or repayment mortgage.
2. The interest rate.
3. Whether there are any incentives.

Interest Only or Repayment

Interest Only Mortgage

This mortgage is self-explanatory – you pay the *interest only* on the balance. So, for example, if you buy a house for £100,000 with a 5% deposit, then you have to borrow £95,000. You will pay the interest charged on this balance only for the duration of the mortgage – usually 25 years. At the end of the 25 years you have to pay back the £95,000. Borrowers usually pay this balance by either selling the property or by cashing in a savings plan maturing at the same time as when the mortgage balance becomes due.

I would recommend anyone who is trying to get on the property ladder to strongly consider interest only mortgages. Choosing this mortgage ensures the lowest monthly payment. My mortgage is an interest only mortgage so I can afford the payments. Having a repayment mortgage can increase payments by up to 25%. I have no savings plan as I intend to move house, rent the existing house out and then sell it at a later date.

Do not worry if people tell you that you will never own your home. It is unlikely that the house you buy first is the house you will be living in in 25 years. The likely scenario is that you will sell the first house you buy within five years to buy the next. The benefit of the positive cashflow over these five years far outweigh the extra interest you pay for those five years. Only when you have found the property you wish to live in for the rest of your life do you ever consider a repayment mortgage.

Repayment Mortgage

This is where you pay interest and a fraction of the capital back in one monthly payment. So for example if an interest only mortgage is £300 per month and the repayment mortgage is £400 per month for the same amount borrowed then the capital repayment is £100 per month.

The capital repayment is a discretionary cost. You can either pay it or not! Why pay it if you can put this £100 to better use? Good uses for this extra £100 would be for improving your property, paying off credit cards or saving it to make other investments such as stocks and shares. Only ever consider a repayment mortgage when you have found your ultimate dream home.

The Interest Rate

There are only two types of interest rate – fixed or variable. There are various sub-categories of this in the table below.

	Type	Narrative
Fixed	Fixed	This is for the low risk-taker. It ensures that the monthly mortgage payment is fixed for a period of time, usually between one to ten years.
	Capped	This is also for a low risk-taker. It ensures that the mortgage payment never exceeds a certain amount but if interest rates fall then your mortgage payment can fall. No downside risk and only upside potential!

Type		Narrative
Variable	Tracker	This is where the interest rate being charged follows the exact rate being set by the Bank of England + an interest loading, typically 1–2%. You are fully exposed to the Bank of England interest rate fluctuations.
	Discount	This is where the initial interest rate is discounted by 1-4% for a specified period of time. This could be a discount on a tracker or a standard variable rate. You are exposed but because there is a discount in place you don't feel the fluctuations quite as badly.
	Stepped	This is where the discount is reduced over a number of years. So you would be entitled to a 3% discount in year 1, 2% discount in year 2 and 1% discount in year 3 for example.
	Variable	This is just the standard variable rate set by the lender. Your mortgage payments are fully exposed to interest rate fluctuations.

You have to be careful of the tie-in/lock-in periods that may exist with all these products. These are the minimum periods that you have to remain with the lender without incurring financial penalties if you wish to redeem the loan because you want to sell or remortgage the property. These are called redemption penalties.

Whether There Are Any Incentives

There are three key incentives to mortgages:

1. Cash-back
2. Valuation and/or solicitors' fees refunded
3. Flexible

Cash-back

The first mortgage I got was a cash-back mortgage. It means you get cash back when you complete the purchase. It ranges between 1% to 10% of the amount borrowed. There is invariably an extended tie-in with these with the penalty being the full repayment of the cash-back given when the mortgage was taken out.

Valuation and/or solicitors' fees refunded

Because lenders are desperate for your business they will even pay for all the fees associated with buying a house. This includes the initial valuation fee, solicitors' costs, arrangement fees and if you are lucky a small cash-back to help with the moving costs.

Flexible

This is a great new introduction to the mortgage market. It enables you to offset all your savings and income against your mortgage. The result is that you save on interest costs due to your savings reducing the overall balance of your mortgage.

Choosing the Right Mortgage

Even though the mortgage you will be able to get will depend on your status ranking you will still have a choice. The higher up the status ranking you are the wider the choice. Guidance is needed on making this choice. The choices will be:

1. Interest only or repayment mortgage.
2. Type of interest rate.
3. Whether you need any incentives.

The choice of mortgage is common sense as long as you have thought about the following things:

- your attitudes to risk
- the type of property
- how much of your income you want to spend on your mortgage
- when you think you are going to move
- degree of aftercare
- the purchase price
- money needed after completion.

By thinking about these seven factors you can build your profile. Let's look at these factors in more detail.

Your attitudes to risk

The risk is that the interest rate rises so the mortgage payment becomes unaffordable. To mitigate this risk you simply go for a fixed rate. If you are willing to accept a degree of risk you go for a capped rate. If you are quite open to risk then you go for a good standard variable rate. See above for the definitions.

The type of property

Lenders have certain exclusions based on the type of property it is. The key exclusions are:

1. **Studio flats** These are flats that have one main room that is used as a lounge and bedroom, plus a kitchen and a bathroom. They are excluded as they can be difficult to sell if there is a property price slump.

2. **Ex-local authority houses and flats** These are properties that were once owned by the local council and subsequently sold on to private people. They are excluded as they are associated with the lower end of the property market.

3. **Flats above commercial properties** These are excluded as the commercial property below could be let out to an Indian or Chinese take-away at some later date. Because of the smell of the food it would lead to a decline in the market value of the property.

4. **Flats with more than four storeys** These will be considered as a high rise block and at the lower end of the property market.

5. **Multiple title properties** These are properties where a freehold exists with a number of long leases and you are trying to buy the freehold. An example of this is a block of flats.

6. **Non-standard construction** If a house is not built with bricks or does not have a pitched tile roof it is deemed non-standard. For example some houses may be constructed from poured concrete. Despite being perfectly fine houses, lenders may consider these properties inferior to the standard construction properties.

How much of your income you want to spend on your mortgage

If you want to spend only, £300, say on your mortgage payment then you go for a mortgage that can do this for you. You can opt for an attractive discount rate that reverts to the standard rate when you know that you would have had a pay rise in that time period. Or you can go interest only which keeps the payment within your budget.

When you think you are going to move

If you intend to move after three years then avoid a mortgage that has a tie-in period greater than three years. This avoids an expensive redemption penalty when you sell the property.

Degree of aftercare
If you want face-to-face communication with your lender then only go for high street lenders that have branches in your area.

The purchase price
Almost all lenders have a minimum purchase price. The minimum purchase price starts at £6,500 and rises up to £75,000 for certain lenders. If your purchase price is below their minimum purchase price then the lender will not consider you under any circumstances.

Money needed after completion
If you want to redecorate your new place then you will need cash. You can create cash by getting a cash-back mortgage or save cash by taking advantage of the lender paying for all the fees for valuation and solicitors' costs.

So a typical profile might be:

Your attitude to risk
Low. Go for a capped or even fixed rate mortgage.

The type of property
Ex-local authority house. Make sure you go for a lender that accepts ex-local authority houses.

How much of your income you want to spend on your mortgage
£400. Ensure that the mortgage payment does not exceed £400. This may involve going for a discounted rate of interest only if the purchase price is high.

When you think you are gong to move.
Three years. Ignore all mortgages that have greater than a three-year tie in.

Degree of aftercare
Low. Non-high street lenders are suitable thus able to get better rates.

The purchase price
Minimum £45,000, Maximum £60,000. Ignore all lenders with mini-

mum valuation below £45,000.

Money needed after completion:
£1,000. Could go for a fee-free mortgage or for a cash-back mortgage of at least £1,000.

So with your typical profile and your status ranking you can pretty much narrow down the right mortgage for you.

5
Increasing Your Buying Power by Increasing Your Status Ranking

Introduction

I showed you in Chapter 2 how to increase your buying power. In summary it was:

1. Increasing your deposit you actually have
2. Increasing the mortgage you're able to get

This is in effect increasing your status ranking. Status ranking is made up of three factors:

a. Your level of savings
b. Your level of income
c. Your creditworthiness

So you have to increase any, some or all of the above to increase your status ranking. Below is how you increase these factors thus increasing your buying power.

Your Level of Savings

You need cash to put down for a deposit. So you need to raise cash to put in the bank. You can do this in one of three ways:

1. Liquidise assets you have now
2. Save some of your income you earn now
3. Take on another job or work more hours

Liquidise Assets You Have Now

Here is a list of assets that you may have that have some value to someone. That is to say that you could sell, liquidise or cash in on these assets and raise cash, as there is a ready market for these type of assets. The best places to advertise these items are in the local press, internet or papers such as *Loot* or *Ad-Trader*. If you cannot be bothered then take the items to dealers in your area.

Cars

How important is the car you have for your day to day activities? Do you commute to work by public transport Monday to Friday, drink at the weekends and only use the car to ferry your weekly household shopping? Have you ever considered getting a taxi or shopping on-line? All the major supermarkets offer on-line shopping – some offer free delivery.

If the car's not that important you can raise cash from the sale of the car plus save on the ongoing running and maintenance costs. Running a car costs anywhere from £50 to £500 per week. This can easily rise to above £1,000 if you take in to account the HP payment if it is on HP. Selling a car can have a dramatic impact on cashflow as not only does it raise cash – it saves cash.

If the car is important to you why not consider trading your car in for a cheaper alternative? Consider this – how impressive is it if you've got a top of the range Ferarri but still live at your parents?

Jewellery

Do you have any jewellery that you no longer and never intend to wear? It is a waste to have these items. Look at these items as if they are cash. There are plenty of jewellery shops out there that have cash ready and waiting. Don't worry if all it raises is £150 – its still £150! This all goes in to the kitty. Remember, you've got to start somewhere.

Furniture, Collections and Other Household Goods

Do you own an expensive record collection that you never touch? I know I do – but I don't need the money now! When I was younger though I used to DJ. I would sell my old records (and when I say old, I mean six months out of date) to raise cash to buy up to date records. This kept me getting bookings for gigs.

Unused goods, collections, furniture or other items can just sit there and eventually end up in a boot sale, jumble sale or even worse – the rubbish bin. Do any of your goods that you no longer use have a value now? Not only can you raise cash but you can also de-clutter your living space.

Endowment Policies, ISAs, Stocks and Shares

You could surrender an endowment policy or liquidise a current share portfolio to raise the cash. I do recommend you talk to your financial advisor and stock broker before taking this action as you could be better off holding out on some of these policies or shares. But it could be time to let go of some poorly performing stocks and enter the property arena as so many of the share market investors are doing now.

An ISA can only ever offer you base rate performance. Forget the interest penalties you may incur. The maximum you could lose if you took a full hit on the penalty is £120 of lost interest. Thinking about it, you're better off making £12,000 on a future capital gain on the property you've bought than a measly £120 in interest.

Electrical Equipment

TVs, videos, DVD players and hi-fis are easy ways to raise cash. Also the actual cassettes can raise you more than you think. There are many second-hand exchange type of stores, such as Cash Converters, that will pay you for these types of goods.

Obsolete Items

Look around your house and garage. Is there anything that you don't use? Now does it have value? The best way to gauge if it has value is to ask yourself – how much did I pay for this thing? If it was substantial, say over £100, and you could imagine someone else using it then it is probably worth something to somebody.

Saving Some of the Income You Earn Now

There are really only two core ways of saving money:

a.   Going without i.e. not spending!
b.   Cutting costs i.e. spending less!

Not Spending

I'm not going to bore you about how you should stop smoking, drinking, eating or just simply indulging. What you should do is when you get paid put a certain amount aside so that you cannot get at it. Put it in a separate deposit account, give it to a family member or put it under your mattress – whatever you do, don't spend it! What will happen is that you'll adjust to the new level of spending that you have at your disposal.

Always ask yourself – do I really *need* this item that I'm buying now or do I just *want* it? Is it a need or a want? If it's a luxury item then its probably a want. When I was setting up my business I went without. Here a some of the things that I used to buy when I was at work but went without when I was starting self-employment:

- newspapers and magazines
- use of a whole flat rather than shared accommodation
- CDs
- designer clothes
- meals at restaurants
- nights out in London visiting trendy bars and nightclubs.

It was easy for me to go without. In the back of my mind I knew that if I went without now I would have in the future. This is now the case and I have a lifestyle that most will envy. I hope this inspires you. Remember, saving for a deposit can be very rewarding. When you do actually save enough and buy your first home the results are very tangible, i.e. the labours of your scrimping and saving will result in you owning your very own home!

Spending Less
There are really only five things you can spend your money on:

i.   Food and consumables
ii. shelter
iii. travel
iv. entertainment and clothing
v.   loans and savings plans

Here are some tips on how to cut back on spending on each of these categories:

Food and Consumables
- **Eat in rather than out.** It is so easy to go to down to your nearest

Burger chain, Indian restaurant or Chinese take-away. There's no washing up, it tastes lovely and there is no preparation time involved.

However, you do pay for this! I used to make myself sandwiches in the poor days. Two slices of bread, a bit of lettuce and a chicken slice – total cost 20p! Compare this to an Indian take-away costing £7 at least. Now I'm not saying don't treat yourself. I treated myself to one chicken biryani from my local Indian once a week – but that was it.

Invariably the food you will prepare at home will be healthier too. The irony is that even though I can afford to eat out every night I now choose to eat in as it is healthier. I even look forward to those chicken sandwiches now!

■ **Go round to your mum's!** Now this may not be possible for everyone. It depends on whether she is still alive, you still see her or if you live close to her. The principle is – don't be ashamed to ask for help. My mum quite enjoyed seeing me twice a week (or sometimes more!) and likewise – there's no cooking like your mum's cooking.

Do you have a brother, sister, nan, cousin or good friend who loves to see you? If you let them know what you are doing – trying to get on the property ladder – then you will be surprised, they will be more than willing to help.

Do not think you are a sponger! *Always* remember people who help you get to the top. As thanks my mum now receives an income from me that is in excess of her pension and she doesn't have to do a thing!

■ **Try non-branded goods.** If you understand how supermarkets work then you will try this. A lot of 'own brand' goods are produced by the branded good manufacturers. So sometimes the quality is the same. Now I say sometimes! I have tried some of the non-branded goods and they taste awful but there are some own-branded goods that taste as good if not better than the branded goods. So give it a try. The cost savings can be up to 50%.

■ **Buy one get one free.** Every supermarket does this. They sell goods at no profit or even at a loss to get you through the door. You can use this to your advantage. If you have the time you can go to every major supermarket and capitalise on all of their deals. I have to admit, I never had the time to justify the cost savings. But if you have a family and you are willing to stock up then I would estimate that you can reduce your shopping bill by 40%.

Shelter

- **Rent a room rather than a flat or house.** Having your own living space is a costly thing. It can sometimes drain your monthly income by up to 70% when you take in to account the rent, rates, bills and insurances. Why not consider lodging? I did. It cost me £55 per week and I was able to preserve the cash that I had saved. I lodged for 12 months with someone who is now a good friend, so I could put a deposit down on my first house.

  Do you really need all that space? Could your social life receive a boost from sharing with others? If you can do this then it will have the most dramatic impact on your level of savings out of all the cost savings mentioned here.

- **Switch utilities suppliers.** It's a competitive market out there when it comes to supplying gas, electricity and telephone. Due to deregulation you can save up to 40% on your bills simply by switching and it is an easy thing to do!

  Look out for new tariffs for your mobile phone. Prices have only come down since their introduction and so there will always be a new tariff being introduced that will trump your existing tariff sooner or later.

- **Shop around for contents insurance.** The insurance market is a competitive one. Do not accept the premium you have to pay just because you paid it last year. Get in contact with a good insurance broker to get you the best deal.

  Have you ever considered not getting insurance? Sometimes you can pay a hefty premium to insure not a lot – and even then you don't get a pay out when you make a claim!

- **Consider purchasing second-hand furniture.** What's more impor-tant to you – owning a house or owning nice furniture? If you are serious about wanting to own your own house then you will do whatever it takes to do it. This may mean sitting on a second-hand sofa, sleeping on an old bed and eating off a table that your cousin gave you!

There are many incentives that retailers are offering such as 0% finance, buy now pay later, bank holiday one off sales etc. Do not get tempted! Save the cash now – get the new furniture later. Once you've bought your flat or house then you can start thinking of furnishing it properly.

■ **Sell the car.** Owning and running a car is not cheap. You've got HPI payments, insurance premiums, road tax duty, petrol and oil costs, servicing costs and repairs. That's a lot of expenses! You could save a small fortune if you did sell the car.

Do a feasibility test on the car. Work out how much you spend a month on the car and see if it is greater than if you walked, cycled, took the train or bus and took taxis. If it is – then it is time to sell the car! Remember a car is a luxury item. Public transport is supposed to be getting better and providing better value for money so be brave – get rid of it!

■ **Downsize the car.** Okay, it may not be practical to get rid of the car but how about downsizing it?
  – Consider a smaller car with a smaller engine – this will cut fuel costs.
  – Consider a lower insurance grouped car. Even consider third party only insurance. When was the last time you had an accident? Statistically you are unlikely to have an accident that is your fault if you haven't had an accident in the last five years.
  – Maybe sell the car on HPI and buy a cheap run-around thus saving on the loan repayments.
  – Road tax is reduced by £60 per year if you drive a car less than 1.5 litre.
  – Get the car serviced by a non-main dealer.

■ **Try walking or get a bike!** If you don't have a car but get buses, trains and/or taxis then consider walking or cycling. You will save on the fares *and* it will keep you fit!

Entertainment and Clothing
■ **Shop in the sales, markets and charity shops.** One of my good friend's dad told me that he buys his winter suits in summer and his

summer suits in winter. The key is to get value for money. If you're shopping in a glitzy, air conditioned, fashionable part of town then you are paying for it! All the expensive rents, rates and décor they have to pay for are ultimately paid by you because they charge you a high mark up on the goods sold.

You'll be surprised how well stocked some of the market traders are now. I still get most of my designer clothes from markets and superstores – not New Bond Street in London W1!

- **Think about if it's a need or a want.** As mentioned above you need to always ask yourself if it's a need or a want. Do you really need to see the latest releases at the cinema or can you wait a year when they hit the Sky channels? Is the latest Kylie CD single with all the mixes really necessary or can you wait for her album? Do you really need the extra pair of trousers that are half price in the sale or are you buying them because they're cheap? If you master this thought process alone then half the battle is won.

- **When you go out – don't stay out late!** I find that when I stay out later I spend more. More on drinks, food, taxis and club entrances. Go home early! I'm not saying just stay out for an hour or so but try to arrive early and go home early. You'll find out that you'll come home with some cash in your pocket rather than having to revisit the cash machines on the night out and regretting it later!

- **Look out for the deals bars, clubs, cinemas and restaurants are offering.** The entertainment market is a highly competitive one. Virtually every evening spot has an offer going on. Take advantage of this! Look out for flyers or leaflets available at their premises. Scan the local press for a restaurant trying to drum up a bit more business. Pay close attention to the TV ads when Pizza Hut and others are doing a promotion.

Loans and Savings Plans
- **Switch credit cards and loans to obtain the best deals.** 0% APR for balance transfers – sounds familiar? I'm sure you've heard this so many times that it no longer means anything – but it does! It means that you can save a lot of cash as you pay no interest on your borrowing. Make sure you capitalise on these deals to save you real money. But don't just be

happy with saving money – make an effort to clear these balances! You will run out of credit companies eventually so you do need to clear this type of unhealthy borrowing.

■ **Cash in or freeze payments to endowment policies and pension plans.** Is the endowment policy you are contributing to really going to mature to its estimated value? You could cash it in, raise cash and save cash as you no longer need to contribute to it.

It's the same for pension contributions. You could freeze payments which will result in an instant saving. When I used to work I was tempted to contribute to a pension. But after careful thought I realised that under no circumstances was I going to hand over any of my hard earned cash to a company that would 'play' with it on the stock market, be unsure of how much I would get back and never access until I was of retirement age.

If you want a real pension fund then invest in property, but that's another story – or even a book!

Take On Another Job or Work More Hours
See below, Your Level of Income, for how to increase your income – including working harder! When we earn more we can save more – in theory anyway!

Your Level of Income
I can already hear you – how do I increase my income? Well this depends on you. You need to be assertive, hard working and be just that little bit cleverer than the rest! There are eight ways that I can think of that will instantly increase your income. This does assumes that you have a job or a business in the first place:

■ work extra hours
■ take on another job
■ ask for a pay rise
■ change your job
■ claim all benefits due
■ exchange benefits for cash
■ switch from permanent employment to sub-contractor
■ increase profitability.

See, I told you – it depends on *you*! Let's look at these ways in more detail.

Work Extra Hours

Are there possibilities to do overtime, work weekends or do nightshift work and get paid for it? You'll probably find out that you will get in excess of your normal hourly rate but even if you don't – still do it! If it means you earn more money then it all goes into building a substantial deposit so you can buy your first home.

When I used to work I did overtime but I never took payment. I used to take the time off instead to set up my business which now earns me an income in excess of what I was getting paid when I was at work!

As long as the opportunity of overtime exists then do it and use it for either payment or time to do things that will either make or save you money.

Take On Another Job

Do you do a 9–5 office job and have your evenings free? I know people who work in pubs and nightclubs who have an office job in the day. It's a great way to increase your social circle. It also means you have less time to spend money as you are working! If you find a job that is a bit of fun then it will not seem that you are working day and night.

What about setting up a small business? If you're passionate about vintage clothes then why not start a market stall on a Saturday? If you're a DJ then go down to your local bars and nightclubs and try to get a spot. Even if you don't get paid you'll save on the perks you get like free drinks and entrance costs.

I have a cleaner, Emma, who comes round once a week and I pay her £35 per week. She also has a full-time job and she also cleans two other people's houses. She lives in rented accommodation at the minute but I know that she will own her own house within two years. I know this because she is not afraid of hard work and she is determined to do whatever it takes to get on that property ladder.

Ask For a Pay Rise

The reason why men get paid more than women is largely due to the fact that they ask for more! If you think you are worth more then go knock on your boss's office door and ask for a pay rise. Back your request up with what you have done for the company, market rate for your type of job and the loyalty you have shown to the business.

I employ three people and I have one guy who frequently asks me for a pay rise – and I like that! He's hungry to prove himself so I promise to increase his pay based on results. He's had two pay rises already and he's only worked for me for eight months!

Change Your Job

This is an extreme measure but a valid one. There is no point staying in a job that's below your perceived market rate. It breeds resentment towards your employer and it drains your energy and motivation.

Put your feelers out. Let your friends and family know that you're looking. Scan the newspapers for the latest advertised jobs. Write to companies for which you would like to work. Ring up the personnel department and tell them you want to work for them. So get your CV up to date and start making some moves!

Claim All Benefits Due

The government has a multitude of benefits to claim even if you are working. There is the family tax credit for starters. Families can have both adults working and still be eligible for some form of credit. There is about £1 billion worth of unclaimed benefits every year. You've seen the TV adverts – 'It's money with your name on it!'

Exchange Benefits for Cash

You may have a company car that you use. Employers offer cash alternatives instead of the car. You may find that you can run a car cheaper than the cash alternative hence an instant saving and a positive effect on your income.

Do you get any benefits from your employer that offer a cash alternative and which you could provide to yourself cheaper than them? There is no point having a brand new car and living in rented accommodation!

Switch from Permanent Employment to Sub-contractor

Usually this happens the other way round. If you're a sub-contractor earning £70,000 pa, and good at your job, the company offers you full-time employment for £45,000 pa. For this you get job security and access to employer benefits such as their health and pension benefits. This is an expensive price to pay. In this example, which is a real example as one of my good friends did this, you lose £25,000 for not much. Okay, he'll get a redundancy payment if made redundant but you have to evaluate how likely this is.

It is worth asking your employer, if it is an environment for sub-contractor work, to consider switching you to sub-contractor income from salaried employment. The increase in pay could be quite staggering.

Increase Profitability

This is a book in itself! For those of you who have a business you should always be looking for ways to increase profitability. Some obvious ways are:

- Reducing the hours worked by your staff and doing the work yourself thus saving on wages and salary costs.

- Pushing more sales through existing customers thus increasing turnover.

- Advertising for more business thus increasing turnover.

- Negotiating harder with your suppliers to reduce costs of sale.

- Switching banks which are offering lower costs of borrowings thus reducing bank and interest charges.

It all depends on your business and how practical this is. But it is worth a thought. Look over all the lines of your profit and loss account and see if you can either increase turnover or decrease expenditure or even both!

So you can see that there are many ways of increasing your income. But if none of the above gets you going then read Chapter 6 Increasing Your Buying Power *Without* Increasing Your Status Ranking to find out how to increase your buying power without having to increase your income.

Your Creditworthiness

Your creditworthiness can be split into two:

1. Your past
2. The present

Your Past

There may be an incorrect entry on your credit file. A credit reference agency must investigate your claim that the record is incorrect. If you believe there are incorrect entries, contact the agency immediately and try to give as much proof as possible in order to back up your argument. For example, send copies of any correspondence you had with that lender. If you believe a CCJ has been incorrectly registered, contact your local County Court.

You may have a legitimate outstanding CCJ that you have not paid. You need to satisfy these before anything else. Contact the creditor and arrange to pay this CCJ off as lenders ask you to distinguish between satisfied and unsatisfied CCJs. You will see from the Reference Chapter that there are many lenders that allow CCJs. There are limited lenders for unsatisfied CCJs so it is in your interest to pay these off to open up a larger number of lenders.

The Present

Lenders will look at your current income and expenditure and make a judgment as to whether you can afford repayments on a loan. If they feel that you have insufficient funds to do so it may be time to repay some of those loans.

Consider clearing store cards, credit cards and unsecured loans so that when your case is presented to the lender they can see that you are not strapped up with unmanageable loans and that you can afford the mortgage payments. The names and addresses of these agencies can be found in the Reference Chapter.

Credit Repair Companies

When lenders refuse you credit it may be tempting to turn to a credit repair agency. Do not do this under any circumstances! These agencies can actually make your situation worse than it now is.

Credit repair agencies claim that you can have County Court Judgments (CCJs) or any other records removed – this is completely untrue. This can only be done if they were incorrectly registered or if the action against you has been discharged. However, there are legitimate ways in which Judgments can be set aside – for example if the judgment is paid within a month or if the person did not receive the relevant summons.

Credit repair companies are unable to do anything that you could not do yourself! In a report published by The Office of Fair Trading, credit repair companies are seen as bogus brokers trying to sell you an adverse credit loan.

6
Increasing Your Buying Power *Without* Increasing Your Status Ranking

Buying Power

Let me remind you of what buying power is:

> BUYING POWER = (deposit you actually have)
> + (mortgage you're able to get)

I showed you how to increase buying power by increasing your status ranking in Chapter 5. This involved, amongst other things, increasing your deposit by saving, increasing your salary by working harder and increasing your creditworthiness by redeeming credit card debt. This all seems like too much effort! There are easier ways to increase your buying power.

I have identified the following ways to increase your buying power without having to increase your status ranking:

i. Vendor incentives – vendor gift or cash-back

ii. Get a guarantor

iii. 100 + % loan to value mortgages

iv. Unsecured loans

v. Get a partner

vi. Self-certification mortgages – no proof of income

vii. High income multiple mortgages

viii. Shared ownership schemes

Vendor Incentives – Vendor Gift or Cash-back

This is where you basically get the mortgage lender to pay most of your deposit! This is best explained by the following example of vendor gift below:

Gavin wishes to buy his first property for £54,000 but he has no money for a deposit.

	Without vendor gift £	With vendor gift £
Purchase price	54,000	60,000
Deposit required (assume 10% of purchase price)	5,400	6,000
Gavin's actual investment	0	0
Shortfall of investment = deposit required minus Gavin's actual investment	5,400	6,000
Vendor contribution = inflated purchase price minus purchase price	N/A	6,000
Actual shortfall = shortfall of investment minus vendor contribution	5,400	Nil

Without vendor gift Gavin has a shortfall of £5,400 so he cannot buy the property.

With vendor gift Gavin has no shortfall. The vendor gets:

$$£60,000 - £6,000 = £54,000$$

The inflated purchase price - vendor contribution = original asking price.

Gavin gets:

His first property costing £54,000 for no money down. His borrowings are however greater than 90% loan to value. His borrowings are 90% of £60,000 = £54,000. This equates to 100% loan to value. In effect Gavin is borrowing all of his deposit from the mortgage lender. Note he is not borrowing any of the deposit from the vendor as the vendor has got his full asking price of £54,000. The vendor deposit figure is purely a notional figure. So Gavin's buying power has risen from nil to £54,000 without changing any level of his deposit, income or creditworthiness.

This trick is completely legal but relies on the property being valued up to £60,000. This is likely because of three reasons:

- **Valuers do not like to down-value a property** – unless there is something wrong with it! If they think the purchase price is only slightly higher than what it is worth they will always value it at the purchase price. This is because the valuer knows that valuations are not an exact science. Valuations are based on what people will pay for a property and he will assume that if you are willing to pay £60,000 then the property is probably worth £60,000. A 10% gross inflation of the purchase price is not a lot considering you are only talking about an inflation of £6,000. For higher value properties (greater than £200,000) I would suggest a 5% vendor deposit contribution as £10,000 purchase price inflation could be contested.

- **You may be getting a bargain property** – i.e. the property is worth £60,000 but you are actually getting it for £54,000, hence it values up to £60,000.

- **Valuers are under pressure to value properties at the purchase price** – lenders make money by lending money. If they instruct a firm of valuers that keep on down-valuing properties then it becomes difficult for the lender to lend and hence make money. The more the valuer values property at the purchase price the more money the lender makes. Especially in the current rising property price conditions, even if the valuer thinks that the purchase price is 1% or 2% inflated he will assume that it will reach the valuation in a few months anyway.

Cash-back works in the same way. In the above example the deal would be structured as:

$$£60,000 \text{ purchase price } + £6,000 \text{ cash-back.}$$

So when you buy the property you put down £6,000 as your deposit, which you may have borrowed on your credit card, and get £6,000 back when you complete the purchase enabling you to pay back your credit card company.

There are tax issues. The vendor has to declare the inflated sales price to the Inland Revenue and thus will have to pay more capital gains tax as his gain is deemed to be higher. For the vendor this may not be a problem as the Inland Revenue gives you an allowance in excess of £7,000 for a capital gain. If this inflated price does not take the gain above this allowance then there is no increased capital gains tax to pay.

Get a Guarantor

You can get a mortgage beyond your affordability limits by getting a guarantor. A guarantor is liable for the mortgage payments and whole balance in the event of your default. A guarantor guarantees that you are a good bet. There are mortgage companies that will grant you a mortgage if you have a guarantor that has good credit. They simply credit check the guarantor as well as you and consider whether your guarantor could pay the mortgage in the event of your default.

The key points are that:

- The maximum mortgage available is calculated on the guarantor's income less existing commitments.

- The guarantor must have good family ties with the applicant and be able to demonstrate the ability to cover their own financial commitments together with the applicant's total mortgage commitment.

- The lender's normal income criteria is applied to assess the mortgage, but by using the guarantor's income as a basis for the maximum loan.

- The lender will make an assessment of the main applicant's future earnings potential, to ensure that the loan applied for can be covered without the guarantor's support later in their career.

- The guarantor can be released at any time providing the borrower's income covers the outstanding mortgage.

So for example, Richard, a young graduate who earns £15,000 pa, could get a mortgage of £100,000 if his parents acted as guarantors and if his income was set to rise to £25,000 within five years. This could be likely if he was a graduate trainee and qualifying in three years after all his professional exams i.e. like an accountant or solicitor. So Richard's buying power has increased from £60,000 (being $4 \times £15,000$) to £100,000 ($£25,000 \times 4$, assuming he will be earning £25,000 within five years).

A list of guarantor mortgages can be found in the Reference Chapter. You can also ask any lender if they would consider taking on a guarantor as this part of the market is relatively new. There will be more introductions of these types of mortgage in the future.

100%+ Mortgages

Having a deposit is advisable as there are more products available to you. If you find saving too painful then there are mortgage companies that will lend you the whole amount. There are even lenders out there that will loan more than the value of the purchase price. The excess amount over the purchase price can be used to improve the property thus pushing up the value of the house. So your buying power can go from £nil, due to the fact that you think no one will lend to you, to £250,000, the maximum 100% + loan to value mortgage you can get. This is best explained with an example.

Joanne, who has no deposit, decides to buy a property for £100,000 but the kitchen and bathroom are in poor repair. She gets an estimate for the work and she finds a builder who will do the complete job for £5,000. Joanne decides to go for the property and apply for a 105% mortgage. This will mean that she will get:

- £100,000 to purchase the property
- £5,000 to repair the property.

After the repair the property will be worth £110,000 as it is more saleable now as the property is more presentable to the market. Thus her buying power has increased from £nil to £110,000 due to the fact that Joanne took on a mortgage that was greater than 100% loan to value.

A list of all the 100% + mortgage providers can be found in the Reference Chapter.

Unsecured Loans

As I have said earlier having a deposit is advisable. You can get one instantly by simply borrowing it! I would suggest that you only take on this credit (if you are borrowing from a credit card or bank) after your mortgage application has been submitted and you have been credit checked otherwise this borrowing will show up.

You can get the deposit from the following sources.

Credit Card Companies

Credit card companies have had a lot of bad press in the past and present and will continue to in future for as long as they're around. The reason for a bad press is not because *they* do anything wrong, it's the *cardholder* who does wrong.

Certain cardholders spend the credit granted on items but have no plan for how they will pay the credit card company back. Is this the fault of the credit card company or the cardholder? I would say the cardholder. Others would say these companies give credit cards to anyone and they make it too easy. Making it easy is a good thing! Why make something hard if you can make it easy?

The key to playing the credit card game is having a plan to pay them back. Many businesses have been funded by credit cards during the bad times and have saved companies going bankrupt – but you never hear about it in the press as it doesn't make good news. I have several credit cards with a total credit limit of £13,000 which will only ever be used if really needed. I used my credit cards a couple of years ago to buy a really cheap investment property as they advance you the cash immediately. Careful use of my credit cards made me £15,000 profit!

Credit card companies are begging us to borrow. So much so that they offer 0% for balance transfer. A list of these is in the Reference Chapter. The trick to obtaining your deposit for your first home is to:

- apply for and obtain a standard credit card
- withdraw cash on this card to the full amount
- apply for and obtain a 0% APR credit card
- transfer the balance on the standard card to the 0% APR card
- pay off the balance before the introductory period is over
- If the introductory period expires apply, obtain and transfer the balance to another 0% APR card.

You have to start this process after you have submitted your application form and you have been credit checked by the mortgage lender.

But please, please, please note: credit cards are expensive when you either default or go over the introductory period. Have a plan for how you are going to pay back this balance and for how long. If you do not then you can end up in unmanageable debt and then owning your own house with all its associated debts will become a nightmare. (Barclaycard offer a lifetime period of 0% until the debt is repaid but this requires you to have a minimum spend per month.)

One way to plan the repayment of the credit card balance is to take up a cash-back mortgage or a 100% + mortgage which gives you cash when you buy the property on completion.

Overdraft Facilities

It's the same principle as the credit card trick above. You simply obtain the deposit from your overdraft provider and pay it back within a set time period.

You may be able to get an overdraft facility from your bank. Simply ask! They will need to see your salary being deposited every week or month for at least six months. This should not pose a problem if they have been your bank for more than six months.

Unlike credit cards banks do not offer introductory rates. They usually start from 5% above Bank of England base rates so at today's rates they start from 8.5% and can rise to 15% so they do work out expensive. The beauty of an overdraft is that it can be redeemed whenever you want to. A good way to redeem it is as above with a cash gift mortgage like cash-back or 100% + mortgage.

Personal Loans

You can raise the deposit by simply taking out a loan. The loan will be paid back over a number of years in equal instalments. You have to consider whether you can pay back the loan and the mortgage in total otherwise there is no point! So for example if you need £5,000 to put down for a £95,000 mortgage then your total cost of borrowings would be:

£5,000 loan	£111.45
£95,000 mortgage	£412.98
Total	**£524.43**

So make sure you can afford both repayments. Unlike the credit cards and overdrafts a loan is less easy to redeem as there are penalties. Sometimes the penalties are not too extortionate so it may be well worth redeeming the loan with penalty to save on interest you will pay over the duration of the loan.

Be sure to apply for the loan after submission of your mortgage application form.

Loan from Friend or Family

I have been on both sides of this equation! I have borrowed and I have lent. In the first instance I borrowed £500 from my Mum to kick-start my first property purchase from my Mum. In the second instance I lent £1,800 to one of my good friends to clear their credit card debt. This friend immediately paid me back using his credit card cheque book when the mortgage completed!

You'd be surprised how helpful the people around you are. I would suggest approaching your family members first and then move outside of the family once all avenues have been exhausted.

Buying power is increased due to deposit levels being increased. The size of the buying power increase can be many hundreds of thousands of pounds especially if you could not buy unless you had a deposit.

Get A Partner

I'm not saying go out and get married to the next person you see or move in with your partner who you are quite frankly unsure about. I just want to show you how a partner, be it a romantic interest or simply a friend or family member, can increase your buying power.

Taking on a partner can have the following effects depending on the status of the partner and also has the following drawbacks.

Status of Partner
Partner with an income and/or deposit.

Buying power effect
The deposit level increases due to the addition of their deposit. See Chapter 5 on the effects of having more of a deposit.

The amount of borrowing available increases due to the addition of their income. See Chapter 5 on the effects of having more of a deposit.

Overall buying power increases due to the two impacts above.

Drawbacks
1. Loss of full freedom of sole ownership. When you have to sell you will need to get the partner to agree on whether you both want to sell and the price.

2. The gain on the property will have to be shared with the partner involved.

3. You will be liable for the mortgage payments if the other partner defaults.

I am involved in a TV programme which will be exactly about this concept. It will be following first-time buyers who have been put together so that they can purchase their first home together and sell within two years, make a gain, split the gain and then use this gain to buy their own property individually. You could use a partner in this way where you both mutually benefit. It is worth planning the exit route and only enter into this type of agreement with people you trust.

Self-Certification Mortgages – No Proof of Income
Lenders can be awkward when it comes to proving your income. If you are self-employed and get paid in cash it can be sometimes difficult to prove your income. If your accountant is not chartered or certified, or you have prepared the accounts yourself, then the lender may point blank refuse to accept that you have earned that income.

With self-certified mortgages the lender does not require proof. You simply self-certify your income. Now this does not mean you lie! It means that they will rely on what you say you earn to lend to you. There is no point in getting a mortgage that you cannot afford!

Self-certified mortgages require a minimum deposit level of 10% so it is key to raise a deposit by either saving or the ways listed above. Buying power is increased from nil to something even though you cannot prove your income!

If you do require your accounts to be certified by a qualified accountant then contact Accountants Direct on (01279) 833 833. They will be happy to do this with limited supporting documentation. Visit www.accdirect.co.uk for more information.

The best self-certified lenders can be found in the reference chapter.

High Income Multiple Mortgages

Instead of going for the standard 3.5 times single income or 2.75 times joint income you can go to the more flexible lenders that offer up to five times single salary + second income. In the Reference Chapter there is a list of lenders who offer greater than four times salary.

This increases your buying power due to the lender offering to lend more than the normal income multiple.

Shared Ownership Schemes

There are many housing organisations that offer you a part buy of their homes. So you can buy, say, 50% of the home and pay a subsidised rent on the other 50%. You then simply only need to get a mortgage for 50% of the value of the house. So for a house worth £200,000 of which you wanted to buy 50% you would only need a mortgage for £100,000.

This way you get to live in a £200,000 house with only a £100,000 mortgage.

Combining a Number of these Tricks to Quadruple Buying Power

So, for example, if you earn £20,000 and have a deposit of £5,000 then under standard terms you could buy a property for:

$$£5,000 + (3.5 \times £20,000) = £75,000$$

If you took a bit of advice from above you could:

a. take on a partner earning £25,000
b. use £10,000 from a credit card
c. go for a high income multiple mortgage
d. go for a 50% shared ownership house

Then you can borrow:

$$£5,000 + £10,000 + (5 \times £25,000) + £20,000 = £160,000$$

Original deposit + credit card loan + (5 × 1st applicant's salary)
+ second applicant's salary = buying power

You could then buy a house worth £320,000 on a 50% shared ownership.

So you can see that buying power has increased from £75,000 to £320,000 without increasing your status ranking!

If you decided not to go for the shared ownership scheme you could still raise your buying power from £75,000 to £160,000 which is still more than double.

And if you decided not to take on a partner your buying power still rises from £75,000 to £230,000.

7
Getting Value for Money

Whenever we buy something, however small, we always want value for money. If we are going to make the biggest purchase we'll ever undertake, like a house, then we would be foolish not to expect this same value for money. There's nothing worse than living in a house that you felt that you got stung on.

My definition of value for money in property is:

*to buy a property that fits as many of your criteria
with the buying power you have.*

Or in other words:

A lot for not a lot!

So how do you do this? Let's assume that you have already set out your criteria for the type of property you want. (I'm not going to bore you and tell you that you should only go for properties with gas central heating, be close to a school or have off-street parking – this is a personal choice and I hope you would have thought about this already so I won't patronise you!) This may be a two-bed flat or house with an en-suite bathroom not more than 1 mile from the train station. Then you can get this type of property and value for money by:

1. Looking for properties that are not advertised in estate agents' windows
2. Buying a property that needs renovation
3. Buying a property outside of your chosen criteria

I would suggest that you follow this method in order. That is to say, if you can't find the property that is not advertised normally then consider buying a property that needs renovation. If you can't find a property that needs renovation then consider altering your criteria. Let's look at this in more detail.

Looking for Properties that Are Not Advertised in Estate Agents' Windows

Three out of four properties are sold by estate agents. That means that one out of four properties are not! So how do you get to buy these properties, where do you look and where do they get sold?

Where to look

■ **Local and national newspapers**

Every local newspaper has a property section. If you look at the back there are houses for sale by private individuals. So why do people sell their house privately? This is because estate agents are expensive. They charge up to 1.5% + VAT of the purchase price. So if you have a house for sale for £200,000 and you are not VAT registered the total cost for an agent to find you a buyer could be up to £3,525. Compare this to the cost of placing an ad for £10!

So flick through the locals and see what's there. Also you could run an ad in the wanted section of the property part of the paper. Simply say what you want with the maximum price you are willing to pay.

National newspapers also have a property section. The *Times* on a Friday and the *Sunday Times* have a very thorough property section. Also the *Daily Express* is a very property focused paper for a reason I'm not quite sure about!

■ **Property auctions**

This is where repossessions, run down properties and council sell-offs are sold off to property investors. So why leave all the bargains for the property investors – we'll have some of that!

There is a list of auction houses in the Reference Chapter. The golden rule of buying from auctions is to have a price limit and stick to it! Auctions can be very exciting knowing that within an hour you could be going home with the home of your dreams. So do not get bowled over with the atmosphere of the auction.

I've never bought from auction houses but I have bid at some. I did break the golden rule, and I did bid higher than my price limit but I was still unsuccessful. So it can even happen to the so-called experts!

Death estates

When someone dies and they have property they usually leave it to their next of kin, being their son or daughter. If the son or daughter no longer lives in the area the property becomes a burden rather than an asset. They need to insure it, maintain it and be responsible for the letting of it with all the problems that letting properties brings.

Sometimes the son or daughter is looking for a quick sale just to get rid of the property. This is where, if you can move fast and have your finance in place, a bargain can be had. So where do you find properties like this? The solicitor handling the death estate will know of this type of property. You should make contact with all the solicitors in the area of your choice that deal will probate death estate work. Explain to them that you are a cash buyer as you have all the finance in place.

Internet

The internet is a great source of properties for sale. Admittedly the majority of the houses for sale on the internet are from estate agents but there are private entries too. Check out www.home.co.uk and www.loot.com. These sites have private individuals selling their own home directly without the use of an estate agent.

Council sell-offs

If you are considering buying in an ex-local authority area then contact the council and ask them if they have any houses they wish to sell. Sometimes councils do not have the finance to renovate some of their property stock so they sell it off instead. Be prepared to have to do some DIY to the house or flat if you are successful in finding something the council wants to get rid of.

Drop leaflets

So after you have made contact with every estate agent in the area and they have not found you anything, it is time to do some hard searching! If you want to own your first property in your chosen area then it requires hard work from *you*. Identify the properties that you like *and* that you think you can afford! Print up some leaflets expressing an interest in the property. The more handwritten they can be the better. Tell people that you want to buy their property and you have the finance to do so.

I'm not saying not to go to estate agents. I have bought virtually all my properties from estate agents and bargains can be had. I am simply offering you an alternative to the standard estate agent.

Buying a Property that Needs Renovation

I'm sure you've seen those property TV programmes about renovating and decorating your property. If you haven't then where have you been! Basically the theory is simple. If you buy a property that needs renovation then the discount you will get is greater than the cost of repair. Let me show you this example.

I bought a seven-bed property for £42,000. I can already hear you say where on earth do you get a seven-bed property for £42,000! I'll tell you. It's in Corby in Northamptonshire. It's a rough council estate and needed a lot of work. All the windows were smashed, the kitchen had been ripped out and the bathrooms were all dated and needed replacing. The total cost of repair was £9,000. It took three months to do. After repair I got it revalued and guess what it revalued at? Not £51,000, but £75,000.

So why does a property become worth more than the cost of a property plus renovation costs? It is simply because people are lazy. People will pay a premium if they can buy a property that needs no work and they can simply move in. My personal property needed complete redecoration. The lady I bought from had a fascination with the colour green and floral wallpaper. There were green carpets, green wallpaper, green kitchen units – it was quite a sight! The property had remained on the market for quite a while. I went in with a low offer and got it accepted. I redecorated the whole house in neutral and modern colours for £5,000. Having paid £240,000 for the house I got it revalued after six months and it valued up to £325,000!

If you are willing to take on a project then you will certainly reap the rewards. The more work you are willing to do the better. But remember – you will be living in a building site for the duration of the renovation.

Buying a Property Outside of Your Chosen Criteria

Area

If you're looking to move in to Knightsbridge, London and have celebrity neighbours, but you earn £25,000 pa, then you'll probably find there are no properties on the market that you can afford! If you cast your net further afield you may find somewhere that you can afford.

I wanted to move to Epping, Essex but the houses that I wanted were all £400,000 + . I found a nice house in the next town along for £240,000 that met all of my criteria apart from the area.

Do not get stuck on one area. Some areas are fashionable and carry a heavy premium. You could buy a house with a garden down the road for the same price as a studio flat in the fashionable area. There may be good transport links to your area of choice and, if there is, the place you buy out of the area offers better capital growth than an area that is already fashionable.

In the Reference Chapter is a list of all the affordable areas. These areas are affordable as you can buy a property there for four times average annual salary or less.

Number of Bedrooms

I'm not suggesting that you, your partner and your three children consider living in a studio flat! But if you want an extra bedroom because you want a study then possibly rethink this. The living room may be quite sizeable and you could put your desk in the corner. The house may have an extra reception room that you could use or you could simply put your desk in your bedroom.

The number of bedrooms has a major influence on the asking price of a property. The less bedrooms you require the more affordable the properties become.

Number of Bathrooms and WCs

Okay, you do need at least one! But en-suites, shower rooms and downstairs WCs all cost. If its just you or you and your partner then having a guest bathroom is simply pure indulgence and unnecessary. Remember – this is your first property, you can start dictating luxuries further up the property ladder.

Private or ex-local authority

There are some very nice council estates that are now privately owned. Before Tony Blair became Prime Minister he lived in Islington in one of those four-storey terraced houses. A long time ago these houses were council houses. Now they are all privately owned and are worth over £1m. My first home was in a council estate and I loved living there.

Check out the council estates in the area of your choice. Drive round them and see what feeling you get from them. You can get a lot more for your money compared to a brand new development. The gardens are bigger, the rooms are bigger and the surrounding areas are properly maintained as it is council property.

Flat or house

If you cannot get a house get a flat. If you're not willing to deviate from any of the above then you have to get a smaller property. I know I would rather own a studio flat that was all mine than rent a two-bedroom house that wasn't.

Detached, semi or terraced

If you want a detached house with an acre but only have £100,000 to spend then it ain't going to happen! You're more likely to get a terrace so get your head out of the clouds and come round to the idea. Again this dream house will be yours but you have to climb the property ladder and buying a terrace could be the only way to get on the first rung.

Proximity to workplace, train station or shopping centre

Consider buying near the next train station further out or buy at the next junction of the dual carriageway further out. These transport links were built to be used so use them! It may only make a five-minute addition to your journey.

Gas central heating, double glazing and other improvements

All these improvements can be carried out at a later date when you have the money. If you are looking for a property that's already had all the key improvements that add value to a home done, then you will be paying for it.

Gas central heating, double glazing and nice décor do not cost a fortune. So if you can get a property without these additions you may be getting the property for a bargain price.

Okay, so you've found the perfect home. What happens next? You have to make an offer!

Making an Offer

If you suspect that there will be a lot of interest in the property because it is cheap, do not be afraid to simply offer the asking price. This way there is no to-ing and fro-ing, the deal is done on the day and the property is removed from the market. If the agents get the asking price then there is no need for them to show the property to someone else.

If you've arranged your mortgage then give a copy of the acceptance letter from the lender to the estate agent. This will convince them that you can act quickly, you are serious about buying the property and you are not just someone off the street who has just seen this property and thinks they can buy it without giving it much thought. If you can also show them your bank statement which proves you have the deposit then do so. Anything that will convince the vendor or estate agent that you are serious will make them unlikely to show the property to someone else.

If you suspect that demand is not high for the property but it is still a good buy then ask the agent or vendor how long it has been on the market. If it's been a while then go in low. I would say 75–80% of the asking price. Ask the person, 'has it ever had an offer? What offers have been refused?' Then you will be able to gauge your entry offer. This is assuming you believe the person in the first place! If you have built up a relationship with an estate agent this should not be an issue, but always be wary.

When the offer is accepted they will almost certainly ask your for you solicitor's details. Have your solicitor arranged prior to placing an offer. The agent will then write to your solicitor to confirm the sale and the solicitor will instruct you what to do from then on.

You have to be patient when buying a property. Under normal circumstances the purchase should take no longer than eight weeks from the date your offer was accepted. There are many things that can go wrong with a purchase and sometimes there is nothing you can do about it but sit back and wait. I have listed below some of the things that can go wrong and what, if possible, you can do about it.

Vendor withdraws property from market

If the vendor has decided to keep the property there is nothing you can do about it. If they have decided to sell to someone else then find out the selling price and go in even higher. If the property is worth more then pay it!

Survey fails or undervalues the property

Find out what it failed on. Ask the vendor to remedy the problems. Do not, under any circumstances, offer to contribute to the cost of any remedial work. This is because after they have remedied the problems they may not sell to you and you will find it difficult to get your money back.

If the property has been undervalued it is difficult to persuade the valuer to value it up but it is worth a try. Consider approaching another lender for revaluation or contributing the difference in the purchase price and the valuation.

The mortgage company require further documentation at the last minute but you do not have the documentation or it will take a long time to get it

Kick up a fuss! If they've approved your mortgage but then want further documentation they should have asked for it earlier. Threaten to complain to the Financial Services Authority (FSA). If all else fails try to get a compromise. That is, if they want your mortgage statement to prove you have kept up to date on your mortgage payments in the last 12 months offer them your bank statements for the last 12 months.

The flow of documentation between solicitors is slow or non-existent

Ring your estate agent and get them to chase for you. The agent's wages depend on the sale of the property so they will have an interest in the sale occurring sooner rather than later. Ring your solicitor and ask what the hold up is. Ask your solicitor if there is anything you can do. If you really want the property, you have to be prepared to do some of the acquisition work yourself. If it is proving impossible to get certain documentation from the freeholders when buying a leasehold then consider losing the property. This is because when it comes to selling the property you will probably have the same problems and purchasers will get fed up and pull out.

If things are progressing normally however, then let your solicitor do everything as this is what you are paying them for. Only react when your solicitor has informed you of a problem or you haven't heard anything for six weeks.

It's advisable, prior to exchange of contracts, that you view the property to see that it is still in the state you first viewed it as exchanged contracts are legally binding. If kitchen appliances were included in the sale then check that they still remain there. Check that the carpets and curtains remain and the condition of the property has not deteriorated.

So, I hope you've learnt something from reading this book, most importantly that almost anyone can buy a property with the right knowledge. GOOD LUCK!

Part Two
Reference Section

On the following pages are all the best deals I could find at the time of writing this book and are for illustration purposes only. To get the latest offers available please feel free to contact my broker, Liz Syms from Connect IFA on 01708 443334. And if you mention my name in connection with the book you will receive a discount on all brokerage fees. You can't argue with that!

You can also find current interest rates and deals by visiting www.moneynet.co.uk

100%+ Mortgage Lenders

All the 100% + mortgage lenders. Some offer in excess of 100%. They also offer up to five + times your salary + partner's salary as total borrowings. These lenders are giving it to you on a plate! I've assumed £100,000 purchase price with £100,000 borrowings even though the lenders offer more. Read the notes on each lender to find out how much they lend.

Yorkshire BS

Rate:	3.50% – 1 year, then 4.25% – 1 year. Then variable rate (5.25% currently)
Product type:	Stepped base rate tracker
Amount of mortgage:	£100,000
Property value:	£100,000
Mortgage type:	Repayment
Total cost (for seven years):	£51,416.24

Monthly Costs

Initial monthly payment:	£500.18
Monthly payment at lender's standard variable rate:	£598.64

Set-up Costs

Mortgage indemnity premium:	£3,000
Arrangement fee:	Nil
Less cash-back:	Nil
Net costs:	£3,000
Other incentives:	Valuation fees refunded
	Legal fees refunded

Conditions

Early redemption penalty:	3% within two years
Conditional insurances:	None
How much you can borrow:	Single income: 3.5 times
	Joint incomes: 3.5 times main income plus 2.2 times second income

Additional Features

Ability to overpay, underpay and take payment holidays. Lender charges interest on a daily basis. Free mortgage payment protection insurance for first six months. Lender will use affordability calculation to calculate potential loan size; refer to lender for details. Lender's acceptance is based upon affordability, the income multiples shown above are for guidance only. Minimum age 25. Minimum loan for loans above 95% is £50,000. Scheme is Bank of England base rate (currently 3.50%) for one year then plus 0.75% for year two. £350 contribution towards legal fees on completion.

Northern Rock

Rate:	3.89% – 01/10/2004, then 5.35% – 01/10/2006. Then variable rate (5.49% currently)
Product type:	Stepped fixed
Amount of mortgage:	£100,000
Property value:	£100,000
Mortgage type:	Repayment
Total cost (for seven years):	£50,0473.15

Monthly Costs

Initial monthly payment:	£521.30
Monthly payment at lender's standard variable rate:	£612.86

Set-up Costs

Mortgage indemnity premium:	N/A
Arrangement fee:	£495
Less cash-back:	Nil
Net costs:	£495
Other incentives:	None

Conditions

Early redemption penalty:	2% of original loan on full redemption within three years.
Conditional insurances:	None
How much you can borrow:	Single income: 3.5 times Joint incomes: 3.5 times main income plus 1 times second income or 2.75 × joint income.

Additional Features

Will not lend in Northern Ireland. Free accident, sickness and unemployment cover for three months. Up to 85% loan secured and 30% as an unsecured loan. Scheme is fixed until 01/10/2004 then Bank of England Base Rate (currently 3.50%) plus 1.85% until 01/10/2006. Lender charges interest on a daily basis. Ability to overpay, underpay and take payment holidays.

Scottish Widows Bank

Rate:	3.89% – 30/09/2004, then 4.1% – 30/09/2005, then 4.80% – 30/09/2008. Then variable rate (4.9% currently)
Product type:	Stepped fixed
Amount of mortgage:	£100,000
Property value:	£100,000
Mortgage type:	Repayment
Total cost (for seven years):	£47,304.58

Monthly Costs

Initial monthly payment:	£521.30
Monthly payment at lender's standard variable rate:	£578.20

Set-up Costs

Mortgage indemnity premium:	N/A
Arrangement fee:	£295
Less cash-back:	Nil
Net costs:	£295
Other incentives:	Valuation fees refunded – max £250 Legal fees refunded – max £150

Conditions

Early redemption penalty:	3% of amount until 30/09/2008 plus legal and valuation fees reclaimed within three years.
Conditional insurances:	None
How much you can borrow:	Single income: 3.5 times Joint incomes: 3.5 times main income plus 1 times second income or 3.5 × joint income.

Additional Features

Will not lend in Northern Ireland. Graduate mortgage. Must be over 21 years old and educated to at least degree standard from a recognised United Kingdom university within last seven years. Must have been in permanent employment in the UK in the preceding 12 months prior to application (not currently serving a probationary period). Minimum term five years, maximum 40 years or expected retirement age. Cheque book facility

For all interest rates listed please check the current rate with the provider.

available. Valuation fee refunded on completion. Lender charges interest on a daily basis. Arrangement fee shown is a non-refundable booking fee. Graduate mortgage: lending available up to 102% LTV, additional 2% is on secured basis over a maximum 10 year period. Capital repayments up to 10% allowed each year without penalty (minimum £1,000).

Direct Line Mortgages

Rate:	3.99% – 6 Months, then 4.9% – 2.5 Years. Then variable rate (4.96% currently)
Product type:	Stepped discount
Amount of mortgage:	£100,000
Property value:	£100,000
Mortgage type:	Repayment
Total cost (for seven years):	£48,801.41

Monthly Costs

Initial monthly payment:	£526.79
Monthly payment at lender's standard variable rate:	£581.68

Set-up Costs

Mortgage indemnity premium:	£375
Arrangement fee:	Nil
Less cash-back:	Nil
Net costs:	£375
Other incentives:	Valuation fees refunded

Conditions

Early redemption penalty:	Three months within three years.
Conditional insurances:	None
How much you can borrow:	Single income: 3 times
	Joint incomes: 3 times main income plus 1 times second income or 2.5 × joint income.

Additional Features

Scheme is a 0.97% discount for the first six months then 0.06% discount for remainder of discount period. Ability to overpay, underpay and take payment holidays. Lender charges interest on a daily basis. Lender's acceptance is based upon affordability, the income multiples shown above are for guidance only.

Royal Bank of Scotland

Rate:	4.46% – 01/08/2005. Then variable rate (5.59% currently)
Product type:	Discount
Amount of mortgage:	£100,000
Property value:	£100,000
Mortgage type:	Repayment
Total cost (for seven years):	£51,571.29

Monthly Costs

Initial monthly payment:	£553.02
Monthly payment at lender's standard variable rate:	£618.83

Set-up Costs

Mortgage indemnity premium:	£1,200
Arrangement fee:	Nil
Less cash-back:	Nil
Net costs:	£1,200
Other incentives:	None

Conditions

Early redemption penalty:	None
Conditional insurances:	None
How much you can borrow:	Single income: 3.25 times
	Joint incomes: 3.25 times main income plus 1 times second income or 2.75 × joint income.

Additional Features

1.63% discount off bank's 100% variable rate (currently 6.09%) then after 01/08/2005 reverts to standard variable rate. Lender charges interest on a daily basis. Free accident, sickness and unemployment cover for three months. Higher income multiples for professionals.

Nat West

Rate:	4.49% – 31/08/2005. Then variable rate (5.59% currently)
Product type:	Discount
Amount of mortgage:	£100,000
Property value:	£100,000
Mortgage type:	Repayment
Total cost (for seven years):	£51,379.65

Monthly Costs

Initial monthly payment:	£554.72
Monthly payment at lender's standard variable rate:	£618.83

Set-up Costs

Mortgage indemnity premium:	£1,030
Arrangement fee:	Nil
Less cash-back:	Nil
Net costs:	£1,030
Other incentives:	None

Conditions

Early redemption penalty:	None
Conditional insurances:	None
How much you can borrow:	Single income: 3.25 times
	Joint incomes: 3.25 times main income plus 1 times second income or 2.75 × joint income.

Additional Features

Will not lend in Northern Ireland. 1.10% discount. No valuation fee. Interest calculated daily. Increased income multiples for professionals of up to 5 x professional salary plus 1 × second salary, or up to 2.75 × joint salary for joint applications. Applicants must be a fully qualified member of one of the following professions: medical doctors, pharmacists, opticians, dentists, vets, solicitors and accountants (minimum salary £20,000, minimum age 23 and must meet all standard affordability guidelines).

Sainsbury's Bank

Rate:	4.7%
Product type:	Variable
Amount of mortgage:	£100,000
Property value:	£100,000
Mortgage type:	Repayment
Total cost (for seven years):	£50,601.29

Monthly Costs

Initial monthly payment:	£566.68
Monthly payment at lender's standard variable rate:	£566.68

Set-up Costs

Mortgage indemnity premium:	£3,000
Arrangement fee:	Nil
Less cash-back:	Nil
Net costs:	£3,000
Other incentives:	None

Conditions

Early redemption penalty:	None
Conditional insurances:	None
How much you can borrow:	Single income: 3 times
	Joint incomes: 3 times main income plus 1 times second income or 2.5 × joint income.

Additional Features

Ability to overpay, underpay and take payment holidays. Lender charges interest on a daily basis. The flexible options are exercised by calling Sainsbury's Bank Customer Services. A pre-set limit is placed on each mortgage account at the outset, equivalent to the original loan plus 5% of the valuation of the property. The 'overpayments' and 'ten repayments a year' flexible options may be exercised immediately, the other flexible options may be exercised after three or 24 monthly repayments depending on the original loan to value and provided there has been no breach of the mortgage terms and conditions. Underpayment can be made or further advances taken up to the pre-set limit. Payments can be stopped for a maximum of six monthly instalments or up to the pre-set limit, whichever is

---

For all interest rates listed please check the current rate with the provider.

less. Any previous overpayments or lump sum payments into the account can also be withdrawn. New customers receive 30,000 free Sainsbury's Nectar points every year (in December).

Bank of Scotland Mortgage Direct

Rate:	4.99% – 31/10/2005. Then variable rate (5.55% currently)
Product type:	Fixed
Amount of mortgage:	£100,000
Property value:	£100,000
Mortgage type:	Repayment
Total cost (for seven years):	£54,828.71

Monthly Costs

Initial monthly payment:	£590.68
Monthly payment at lender's standard variable rate:	£624.28

Set-up Costs

Mortgage indemnity premium:	£3,000
Arrangement fee:	£300
Less cash-back:	Nil
Net costs:	£3,300
Other incentives:	None

Conditions

Early redemption penalty:	2% and 1% until 31/10/2005, £150 admin charge thereafter
Conditional insurances:	None
How much you can borrow:	Single income: 3.25 times
	Joint incomes: 3.25 times main income plus 1 times second income or 2.75 × joint income.

Additional Features

Enhanced income multiples available for professionals, doctors, dentists, pharmacists, actuaries, solicitors/barristers, chartered surveyors, chartered accountants, architects and veterinary surgeons. No arrangement fee will be charged for cases direct with lender.

Adverse Mortgage Lenders

There are no 100% + adverse lenders. Adverse mortgage lenders start at
95% i.e. they require a 5%-25% deposit. I have assumed a 25% deposit for
a £100,000 purchase price on all the calculations following.

Irish Permanent

Rate:	3.99% – 6 Months. Then variable rate (4.49% currently)
Product type:	Base rate tracker
Amount of mortgage:	£75,000
Property value:	£100,000
Mortgage type:	Repayment
Total cost (for seven years):	£35,535.34

Monthly Costs

Initial monthly payment:	£399.65
Interest payment at lender's standard variable rate:	£421.06

Set-up Costs

Mortgage indemnity premium:	Nil
Arrangement fee:	£295
Less cash-back:	Nil
Net costs:	£295
Other incentives:	None

Conditions

Early redemption penalty:	None
Conditional insurances:	None
How much you can borrow:	Single income: 3.25 times Joint incomes: 3.25 times main income plus 1 times second income or 2.5 × joint income.

Additional Features

Will not lend in Scotland or Northern Ireland. Scheme is Bank of England base rate (currently 3.5%) plus 0.99% with 0.5% discount for six months. Maximum of two CCJs to a combined value up to £500, must be satisfied for at least two years.

Capital Home Loans

Rate: 3.99% – 6 months. Then variable rate (4.49% currently)

Product type: Base rate tracker
Amount of mortgage: £75,000
Property value: £100,000
Mortgage type: Repayment
Total cost (for seven years):   £35,535.34

Monthly Costs

Initial monthly payment: £399.65
Interest payment at lender's standard variable rate: £421.06

Set-up Costs

Mortgage indemnity premium: Nil
Arrangement fee: £295
Less cash-back: Nil
Net costs: £295
Other incentives: None

Conditions

Early redemption penalty: None
Conditional insurances: None
How much you can borrow: Single income: 3.25 times
Joint incomes: 3.25 times main income plus 1 times second income or 2.5 × joint income.

Additional Features

Will not lend in Scotland or Northern Ireland. Scheme is Bank of England Base Rate (currently 3.5%) plus 0.99% with 0.5% discount for six months. Maximum of two CCJs to a combined value up to £500, must be satisfied for at least two years.

Birmingham Midshires

Rate:	4.09% – 2 years. Then variable rate (4.75% currently)
Product type:	Base rate tracker
Amount of mortgage:	£75,000
Property value:	£100,000
Mortgage type:	Repayment
Total cost (for seven years):	£35,559.94

Monthly Costs

Initial monthly payment:	£399.24
Interest payment at lender's standard variable rate:	£427.16

Set-up Costs

Mortgage indemnity premium:	Nil
Arrangement fee:	£349
Less cash-back:	Nil
Net costs:	£349
Other incentives:	None

Conditions

Early redemption penalty:	5% then 4% within two years
Conditional insurances:	None
How much you can borrow:	Single income: 3.25 times
	Joint incomes: 3.25 times main income plus 1 times second income or 2.75 × joint income.

Additional Features

Lender charges interest on a daily basis. Lender will allow one satisfied CCJ and arrears registered of £250 within the last three years. Minimum term available is five years, maximum term available is 40 years. Loans above £2m are by individual negotiation. Scheme is Bank of England base rate (currently 3.5%) plus 0.59% for two years then 1.25% for term.

Scarborough

Rate:	4.14% – 25 years. Then variable rate (4.14% currently)
Product type:	Base rate tracker
Amount of mortgage:	£75,000
Property value:	£100,000
Mortgage type:	Repayment
Total cost (for seven years):	£33,492.65

Monthly Costs

Initial monthly payment:	£401.70
Interest payment at lender's standard variable rate:	£401.70

Set-up Costs

Mortgage indemnity premium:	Nil
Arrangement fee:	Nil
Less cash-back:	£250
Net costs:	£ − 250.00
Other incentives:	Valuation fees refunded

Conditions

Early redemption penalty:	None
Conditional insurances:	None
How much you can borrow:	Single income: 3.5 times
	Joint incomes: 3.5 times main income plus 1 times second income or 2.85 × joint income.

Additional Features

Will not lend in Northern Ireland. Scheme is Bank of England base rate (currently 3.5%) plus 0.64% (minimum pay rate of 3%). Overpayments, underpayments and payment holidays allowed. Loans above £250,000 are by individual negotiation. Applicants with CCJs will be considered, maximum of two CCJs up to £500 per applicant that have been satisfied within previous 12 months.

Kensington Mortgage Co

Rate:	5.4% – 31/08/2004, then 5.9% – 31/08/2005, then 6.15% – 31/08/2006. Then variable rate (6.4% currently)
Product type:	Stepped discount
Amount of mortgage:	£75,000
Property value:	£100,000
Mortgage type:	Repayment
Total cost (for seven years):	£41,972.37

Monthly Costs

Initial monthly payment:	£461.40
Interest payment at lender's standard variable rate:	£507.65

Set-up Costs

Mortgage indemnity premium:	Nil
Arrangement fee:	£395
Less cash-back:	Nil
Net costs:	£395
Other incentives:	None

Conditions

Early redemption penalty:	6% within three years
Conditional insurances:	None
How much you can borrow:	Single income: 3.5 times
	Joint incomes: 3 × joint income.

Additional Features

Will not lend in Northern Ireland. Rate charged is dependent on applicant's personal circumstances and lender will accept any number of arrears, CCJs etc but rate will be have a higher loading. Scheme is variable (currently 4.65%) plus 1.75% with 1% discount until 31/08/2004 then 0.5% discount until 31/08/2005 and 0.25% discount until 31/08/2006. The maximum this scheme allows is up to £5,000 of CCJs (cleared or not) and one month's arrears in last six months and three payments in last 7–12 months. Involuntary arrangements satisfied one year before application. Bankrupts discharged one year before application. Free accident, sickness and redundancy cover for first three months. Free buildings and contents insurance for the first three months. Also available on a self-certification basis but rate loaded by 0.25%.

For all interest rates listed please check the current rate with the provider.

Home Loans Direct

Rate:	5.45% – 01/08/2005. Then variable rate (5.6% currently)
Product type:	Fixed
Amount of mortgage:	£75,000
Property value:	£100,000
Mortgage type:	Repayment
Total cost (for seven years):	£39,251.80

Monthly Costs

Initial monthly payment:	£457.86
Interest payment at lender's standard variable rate:	£464.58

Set-up Costs

Mortgage indemnity premium:	Nil
Arrangement fee:	£395
Less cash-back:	Nil
Net costs:	£395
Other incentives:	None

Conditions

Early redemption penalty:	6% until 01/08/2005
Conditional insurances:	None
How much you can borrow:	Single income: 3.5 times
	Joint incomes: 3.5 times main income plus 1 times second income or 3 × joint income.

Additional Features

Scheme is fixed until 01/08/2005 then Libor (currently 3.65%) plus 1.95%. Maximum number of CCJs to the value of £3,000. Maximum of two months arrears in last 12 months. Bankrupts or IVA not acceptable. Lender charges interest on a daily basis.

Northern Rock

Rate:	2.49% – 6 Months, then 4.49% – 01/10/2010. Then variable rate (5.24% currently)
Product type:	Stepped base rate tracker
Amount of mortgage:	£75,000
Property value:	£100,000
Mortgage type:	Repayment
Total cost (for seven years):	£34,460.28

Monthly Costs

Initial monthly payment:	£335.84
Interest payment at lender's standard variable rate:	£448.54

Set-up Costs

Mortgage indemnity premium:	Nil
Arrangement fee:	£495
Less cash-back:	£500
Net costs:	£ – 5.00
Other incentives:	None

Conditions

Early redemption penalty:	1% of original loan on full redemption until 01/10/2006. Repay cash-back within three years in full.
Conditional insurances:	None
How much you can borrow:	Single income: 3.5 times. Joint incomes: 3.5 times main income plus 1 times second income or 2.75 × joint income.

Additional Features

Will not lend in Northern Ireland. Scheme is Bank of England base rate (currently 3.5%) plus 0.99% with 2% discount for six months. Rate will be no more than 0.99% above Bank of England base rate until 01/10/2010. Loyalty discount after seven years (currently 0.25%). Free accident, sickness and unemployment cover for three months. Lender charges interest on a daily basis. Capital repayments up to 15% allowed each year without penalty. Ability to overpay, underpay and take payment holidays. Offset mortgage with savings account with the options of connections benefit or connections interest current account with connection benefit. Maximum loan to value for self-certification is 85%.

West Bromwich

Rate:	3.75% – 31/07/2005, then 5.65% – three years. Then variable rate (4.9% currently)
Product type:	Fixed
Amount of mortgage:	£75,000
Property value:	£100,000
Mortgage type:	Repayment
Total cost (for seven years):	£37,156.76

Monthly Costs

Initial monthly payment:	£389.57
Interest payment at lender's standard variable rate:	£439.02

Set-up Costs

Mortgage indemnity premium:	Nil
Arrangement fee:	£295
Less cash-back:	Nil
Net costs:	£295
Other incentives:	Valuation fees refunded – max £325

Conditions

Early redemption penalty:	3% until 31/07/2005
Conditional insurances:	None
How much you can borrow:	Single income: 3.75 times
	Joint incomes: 3.75 times main income plus 1 times second income or 3 × joint income.

Additional Features

Will not lend in Northern Ireland. Free accident, sickness and unemployment cover for six months (for direct cases). Privileged rate applies after five years (currently 4.9%). Free valuation refund (max £325) on direct applications only. Interest rate is reduced by 0.16% if lender's buildings cover taken. Maximum loan available for self-certification is £250,000 and maximum loan to value 75%.

Bristol and West

Rate:	4.05% – 30/09/2006. Then variable rate (5.25% currently)
Product type:	Fixed
Amount of mortgage:	£75,000
Property value:	£100,000
Mortgage type:	Repayment
Total cost (for seven years):	£36,491.14

Monthly Costs

Initial monthly payment:	£402.19
Interest payment at lender's standard variable rate:	£454.63

Set-up Costs

Mortgage indemnity premium:	Nil
Arrangement fee:	£299
Less cash-back:	Nil
Net costs:	£299
Other incentives:	None

Conditions

Early redemption penalty:	5% until 30/09/2006 plus administration fee £100.
Conditional insurances:	None
How much you can borrow:	Single income: 4 times Joint incomes: 4 times main income plus 1 times second income or 2.75 × joint income.

Additional Features

Will not lend in Northern Ireland. Scheme is fixed until 30/09/2006 then Bank of England base rate (currently 3.5%) plus 1.75%. Available on a self-certification of income basis for self-employed applicants who have only been trading for one year. Minimum age of applicants – 21 years. Capital repayments up to 50% allowed each year without penalty. If you do not have gross income of £20k but fit all other standard criteria then income multiples will be 3.5 × main plus 1 × second or 2.75 × joint.

UCB Home Loans

Rate:	4.35% – five years. Then variable rate (5.89% currently)
Product type:	Base rate tracker
Amount of mortgage:	£75,000
Property value:	£100,000
Mortgage type:	Repayment
Total cost (for seven years):	£36,367.37

Monthly Costs

Initial monthly payment:	£410.12
Interest payment at lender's standard variable rate:	£477.70

Set-up Costs

Mortgage indemnity premium:	Nil
Arrangement fee:	£295
Less cash-back:	Nil
Net costs:	£295
Other incentives:	None

Conditions

Early redemption penalty:	Four months within three years then three months within two years
Conditional insurances:	None
How much you can borrow:	Single income: 3.25 times Joint incomes: 3.25 times main income plus 1 times second income or 2.75 × joint income.

Additional Features

Will not lend in Northern Ireland. Scheme is Bank of England base rate (currently 3.5%) plus 0.85% for five years then FlexiPlus rate (currently 5.89%). Ability to overpay, underpay and take payment holidays. Lender charges interest on a daily basis. Self-employed must have been in their current business for a minimum of 12 months.

For all interest rates listed please check the current rate with the provider.

Britannic Money plc

Rate:	4.39% – two years. Then variable rate (5.79% currently)
Product type:	Discount
Amount of mortgage:	£75,000
Property value:	£100,000
Mortgage type:	Repayment
Total cost (for seven years):	£38,470.52

Monthly Costs

Initial monthly payment:	£411.81
Interest payment at lender's standard variable rate:	£473.15

Set-up Costs

Mortgage indemnity premium:	Nil
Arrangement fee:	£199
Less cash-back:	Nil
Net costs:	£199
Other incentives:	None

Conditions

Early redemption penalty:	3% within two years
Conditional insurances:	None
How much you can borrow:	Single income: 3.5 times Joint incomes: 3.5 times main income plus 1 times second income or 2.75 × joint income.

Additional Features

1.4% discount. Current account mortgage allows chequebook/Switch card. Lender charges interest on a daily basis. Ability to overpay, underpay and take payment holidays after three years. Capital repayments up to 10% allowed each year without penalty. Free for six months mortgage payment protection and insurance against illness. Maximum loan to value for self-certification is 85%.

Sun Bank

Rate:	4.40% – 01/07/2005. Then variable rate (5.45% currently)
Product type:	Discount
Amount of mortgage:	£75,000
Property value:	£100,000
Mortgage type:	Repayment
Total cost (for seven years):	£38,242.78

Monthly Costs

Initial monthly payment:	£417.17
Interest payment at lender's standard variable rate:	£463.66

Set-up Costs

Mortgage indemnity premium:	Nil
Arrangement fee:	£395
Less cash-back:	Nil
Net costs:	£395
Other incentives:	None

Conditions

Early redemption penalty:	5% until 01/07/2005
Conditional insurances:	None
How much you can borrow:	Single income: 3.5 times
	Joint incomes: 3.5 times main income plus 1 times second income or 2.75 × joint income.

Additional Features

Scheme Bank of England base rate (currently 3.5%) plus 1.95% with 1.05% discount until 01/07/2005. Capital repayments up to 10% allowed each year without penalty. Available to both employed and self-employed. Term from five years to 35 years. Minimum age 21 maximum 75. Lender's acceptance is based upon affordability, the income multiples shown above are for guidance only.

For all interest rates listed please check the current rate with the provider.

Mortgage Express

Rate:	4.5% – two years. Then variable rate (5.5% currently)
Product type:	Base rate tracker
Amount of mortgage:	£75,000
Property value:	£100,000
Mortgage type:	Repayment
Total cost (for seven years):	£38,396.13

Monthly Costs

Initial monthly payment:	£421.49
Interest payment at lender's standard variable rate:	£465.93

Set-up Costs

Mortgage indemnity premium:	Nil
Arrangement fee:	£325
Less cash-back:	Nil
Net costs:	£325
Other incentives:	None

Conditions

Early redemption penalty:	Six months' interest within two years.
Conditional insurances:	None
How much you can borrow:	Single income: 3.5 times
	Joint incomes: 3.5 times main income plus 1 times second income or 2.75 × joint income.

Additional Features

Will not lend in Northern Ireland. Scheme is Bank of England base rate (currently 3.5%) plus 2% with 1% discount for two years. Scheme available on self-certification basis for self-employed. Self-certification remortgaging/ capital raising between 85%–90% please refer to lender.

Bank of Scotland Mortgage Direct

Rate: 4.5% – 25 years. Then variable rate (4.5% currently)

Product type: Base rate tracker

Amount of mortgage: £75,000

Property value: £100,000

Mortgage type: Repayment

Total cost (for seven years): £35,705.49

Monthly Costs

Initial monthly payment: £421.49

Interest payment at lender's standard variable rate: £421.49

Set-up Costs

Mortgage indemnity premium: Nil

Arrangement fee: £300

Less cash-back: Nil

Net costs: £300

Other incentives: None

Conditions

Early redemption penalty: £150 admin charge

Conditional insurances: None

How much you can borrow: Single income: 3.25 times
Joint incomes: 3.25 times main income plus 1 times second income or 2.75 × joint income.

Additional Features

Scheme is Bank of Scotland base rate (currently 3.5%) plus 1%. Ability to overpay, underpay and take payment holidays (available after first three monthly instalments). Cheque book facility available. Enhanced income multiples available for professionals, doctors, dentists, pharmacists, actuaries, solicitors/barristers, chartered surveyors, chartered accountants, architects and veterinary surgeons. Maximum loan to value for self-certification is 85%, maximum loan £300,000.

Scottish Widows Bank

Rate:	4.59% – 30/09/2008. Then variable rate (4.9% currently)
Product type:	Fixed
Amount of mortgage:	£75,000
Property value:	£100,000
Mortgage type:	Repayment
Total cost (for seven years):	£35,891.29

Monthly Costs

Initial monthly payment:	£420.30
Interest payment at lender's standard variable rate:	£433.65

Set-up Costs

Mortgage indemnity premium:	Nil
Arrangement fee:	£295
Less cash-back:	Nil
Net costs:	£295
Other incentives:	Valuation fees refunded – max £250 Legal fees refunded – max £150

Conditions

Early redemption penalty:	3% of amount until 30/09/2008 plus legal and valuation fees reclaimed within three years.
Conditional insurances:	None
How much you can borrow:	Single income: 3.5 times Joint incomes: 3.5 times main income plus 1 times second income or 2.75 × joint income.

Additional Features

Will not lend in Northern Ireland. Cheque book facility available. Lender charges interest on a daily basis. Payment holidays allowed. Valuation fee refunded on completion. Arrangement fee shown is a non-refundable booking fee. Capital repayments up to 10% allowed each year without penalty (minimum £1,000).

Leek United

Rate:	4.59% – ten years. Then variable rate (5.44% currently)
Product type:	Discount
Amount of mortgage:	£75,000
Property value:	£100,000
Mortgage type:	Repayment
Total cost (for seven years):	£35,055.22

Monthly Costs

Initial monthly payment:	£420.30
Interest payment at lender's standard variable rate:	£457.41

Set-up Costs

Mortgage indemnity premium:	Nil
Arrangement fee:	Nil
Less cash-back:	£250
Net costs:	£ – 250
Other incentives:	None

Conditions

Early redemption penalty:	None
Conditional insurances:	None
How much you can borrow:	Single income: 3.5 times Joint incomes: 3.5 times main income plus 1.5 times second income or 2.75 × joint income.

Additional Features

Will not lend in Northern Ireland or Scotland. 1% discount. Free valuation. Ability to overpay, underpay and take payment holidays with drawdown facility. Interest calculated daily. Self-certification available up to 60% loan to value. Privileged borrower rate (currently 5.44%) after ten years.

Stroud and Swindon

Rate:	5.34% – two years, then 5.09% – three years. Then variable rate (5.09% currently)
Product type:	Stepped discount
Amount of mortgage:	£75,000
Property value:	£100,000
Mortgage type:	Repayment
Total cost (for seven years):	£37,770.48

Monthly Costs

Initial monthly payment:	£453.43
Interest payment at lender's standard variable rate:	£442.38

Set-up Costs

Mortgage indemnity premium:	Nil
Arrangement fee:	£345
Less cash-back:	Nil
Net costs:	£345
Other incentives:	Valuation fees refunded

Conditions

Early redemption penalty:	None
Conditional insurances:	None
How much you can borrow:	Single income: 3.5 times Joint incomes: 3.5 times main income plus 1 times second income or 2.75 × joint income.

Additional Features

Will not lend in Scotland or Northern Ireland. Scheme is 0.25% discount for two years then 0.50% discount for three years then loyalty discount base rate (currently 5.09%). Ability to make lump sums and drawdown funds at later stage. Valuation fees refunded on completion on properties up to £600,000.

For all interest rates listed please check the current rate with the provider.

Kent Reliance BS

Rate:	5.43%
Product type:	Variable
Amount of mortgage:	£75,000
Property value:	£100,000
Mortgage type:	Repayment
Total cost (for seven years):	£37,457.93

Monthly Costs

Initial monthly payment:	£462.76
Interest payment at lender's standard variable rate:	£422.80

Set-up Costs

Mortgage indemnity premium:	Nil
Arrangement fee:	£25
Less cash-back:	Nil
Net costs.	£25
Other incentives:	None

Conditions

Early redemption penalty:	None
Conditional insurances:	None
How much you can borrow:	Single income: 3.5 times
	Joint incomes: 3.5 times main income plus 1 times second income or 3 × joint income.

Additional Features

Will not lend in Northern Ireland or Scotland. Loyalty rate applies after four years currently 4.53%. Early loyalty option available from beginning of year three (subject to terms, refer to lender).

A selection of the rest:

Name	Rate	Max %	Fee	Cash-back	Redemption	CCJs	Arrears
BM Solutions	5.39% fixed until 01/11/2005	90%	£349	Nil	5% until 01/11/ 2004 then 4% and 3% until 01/11/2005	maximum of £5,000 CCJs allowed but no CCJs registered within last six months	maximum of two mortgage payments missed within last 12 months
Bristol and West	5.25% tracker	85%	£299	Nil	5% until 30/11/ 2005 then 4% until 30/11/ 2006 plus fee of £150	unlimited number of CCJs to value £10,000 (none in last six months)	arrears that have not increased over last six months
Bristol and West	6.70% tracker	85%	£299	Nil	6% within three years. One month thereafter plus fee of £185	unlimited number of CCJs	unlimited arrears
Kensington Mortgage	6.65% stepped discount until 31/08/2006	90%	£395	Nil	6% within three years	the maximum this scheme allows is up to £5,000 of CCJs (cleared or not)	one month in last three months, three payments in seven to 12 months
Chelsea	4.94% one year discount	85%	£395	Nil	5%, 4% and 3% within three years	maximum of £5,000	three missed payments in the last 12 months (providing only one in last six months)

For all interest rates listed please check the current rate with the provider.

Best of the Less than 100% Mortgage Lenders

There are loads of lenders willing to lend to you if you've got a 5% deposit or more. There is no point in me listing them all. I've included a selection below that are the best based on their:

a. high income multiples
b. bargain rates
c. flexibility

I've assumed a £100,000 purchase price with a 5% deposit.

Bank of Ireland

Rate:	3.38% – 01/09/2005. Then variable rate (5.54% currently)
Product type:	Discount
Amount of mortgage:	£95,000
Property value:	£100,000
Mortgage type:	Repayment
Total cost (for seven years):	£48,851.42

Monthly Costs

Initial monthly payment:	£474.10
Monthly payment at lender's standard variable rate:	£592.49

Set-up Costs

Mortgage indemnity premium:	£1,790
Arrangement fee:	£299
Less cash-back:	Nil
Net costs:	£2,089
Other incentives:	None

Conditions

Early redemption penalty:	5% until 01/09/2005
Conditional insurances:	None
How much you can borrow:	Single income: 4 times
	Joint incomes: 4 times main income plus 1 times second income or 2.75 × joint income.

Additional Features

For Northern Ireland rates call 01232 241155. 2.16% discount. Income multiples shown are based on an income of £20,000 and clean credit record (refer to lender for full details).

Bristol and West

Rate:	3.64% – 30/09/2005. Then variable rate (5.54% currently)
Product type:	Discount
Amount of mortgage:	£95,000
Property value:	£100,000
Mortgage type:	Repayment
Total cost (for seven years):	£47,319.74

Monthly Costs

Initial monthly payment:	£487.66
Monthly payment at lender's standard variable rate:	£592.49

Set-up Costs

Mortgage indemnity premium:	N/A
Arrangement fee:	£299
Less cash-back:	Nil
Net costs:	£299
Other incentives:	Valuation fees refunded

Conditions

Early redemption penalty:	5% until 30/09/2005 plus £100 for term
Conditional insurances:	None
How much you can borrow:	Single income: 4 times
	Joint incomes: 4 times main income plus 1 times second income or 2.75 × joint income.

Additional Features

Will not lend in Northern Ireland. 1.90% discount. If you do not have gross income of £20k but fit all other standard criteria then income multiples will be 3.5 × main plus 1 × second or 2.75 × joint. Three months free mortgage protection payment insurance available.

Staffordshire BS

Rate:	0.9% – one year, then 3.4% – one year, then 5.44% – three years. Then variable rate (5.04% currently)
Product type:	Stepped discount
Amount of mortgage:	£95,000
Property value:	£100,000
Mortgage type:	Repayment
Total cost (for one year):	£4,539.52

Monthly Costs

Initial monthly payment:	£353.63
Monthly payment at lender's standard variable rate:	£557.01

Set-up Costs

Mortgage indemnity premium:	N/A
Arrangement fee:	£295
Less cash-back:	Nil
Net costs:	£295
Other incentives:	None

Conditions

Early redemption penalty:	5%, 4% then 3% within three years plus fee £199 for term.
Conditional insurances:	None
How much you can borrow:	Single income: 3.5 times Joint incomes: 3.5 times main income plus 1 times second income or 2.75 × joint income.

Additional Features

Direct with lender only. Will not lend in Scotland or Northern Ireland. Scheme is 4.54% discount first year then 2.05% discount second year. Free accident, sickness and unemployment cover for six months. Lender charges interest on a daily basis. Loyalty bonus applies after five years (currently 0.40%) discount.

Northern Rock

Rate: 2.49% – six months, then 4.49% – 01/10/2010. Then variable rate (5.24% currently)

Product type: Stepped cash back base rate tracker

Amount of mortgage: £95,000

Property value: £100,000

Mortgage type: Repayment

Total cost (for seven years): £43,651.02

Monthly Costs

Initial monthly payment: £425.40

Interest payment at lender's standard variable rate: £568.14

Set-up Costs

Mortgage indemnity premium: Nil

Arrangement fee: £495

Less cash-back: £500

Net costs: £−5

Other incentives: None

Conditions

Early redemption penalty: 1% of original loan on full redemption until 01/10/2006. Repay cash-back within three years in full.

Conditional insurances: None

How much you can borrow: Single income: 3.5 times
Joint incomes: 3.5 times main income plus 1 times second income or 2.75 × joint income.

Additional Features

Will not lend in Northern Ireland. Scheme is Bank of England base rate (currently 3.5%) plus 0.99% with 2% discount for six months. Rate will be no more than 0.99% above Bank of England base rate until 01/10/2010. Loyalty discount after seven years (currently 0.25%). Free accident, sickness and unemployment cover for three months. Lender charges interest on a daily basis. Capital repayments up to 15% allowed each year without penalty. Ability to overpay, underpay and take payment holidays. Offset mortgage with savings account with the options of connections benefit or connections interest current account with connection benefit. Maximum loan to value for self-certification is 85%.

Cash-back Mortgages

We talked about the generous mortgage lenders that give you cash, well here they are!

Name	Rate	Max %	Fee	Cash-back	Redemption	Notes
Scarborough	6.29% fixed	85%	Nil	10%	Cash-back repaid within ten years from 100% in the first year reducing by 10% each year until year ten. Also 5% within six years then 4%, 3%, 2% and 1% for next four years of sum repaid	Capital repayments up to 5% allowed each year without penalty
Northern Rock	5.49% variable	95%	£595	7%	7%, 6%, 5%, 4%, 3% and 2% within six years (repay help with cost option within three years)	Capital repayments up to 15% allowed each year without penalty
Alliance and Leicester	5.25% tracker	90%	Nil	7%	7%, 6%, 5%, 4%, 3% and 2% within six years	Intermediary only
Chelsea	5.44% variable	90%	£245	6%	Repay cash-back within six years	Direct or www.thechelsea.co.uk only
Bank of Ireland	5.25% tracker	95%	£299	5%	7%, 6%, 5% and 4% within four years	None
West Bromwich	4.50% discount	95%	£295	5%	Repay cash-back within five years	Privileged rate applies after five years
Principality	5.10% discount	95%	Nil	3%	1% and cash-back until 31/10/2008	None

Mortgage Lenders with Income Multiples Greater Than 4

The following lenders can increase your buying power by simply lending you more than usual:

- Beverley BS
- Scottish Widows Bank
- Halifax

Beverley BS

Rate:	3.75% – two years, then 4.95% – 30/09/2008. Then variable rate (4.95% currently)
Product type:	Stepped discount
Amount of mortgage:	£100,000
Property value:	£150,000
Mortgage type:	Interest only
Total cost (for one year):	£4,045

Monthly Costs

Initial monthly payment:	£312.50
Monthly payment at lender's standard variable rate:	£412.50

Set-up Costs

Mortgage indemnity premium:	N/A
Arrangement fee:	£295
Less cash-back:	Nil
Net costs:	£295
Other incentives:	None

Conditions

Early redemption penalty:	4% until 30/09/2008 (also for remortgages repay cash-back within two years)
Conditional insurances:	None
How much you can borrow:	Single Income: 4.25 times
	Joint Incomes: 4.25 times main income plus 1 times second income or 3.50 × joint income.

Additional Features

Loans above £100,000 are by individual negotiation. Lender charges interest on a daily basis. Scheme is 1.2% discount for 2 years then rate capped at 5.6% until 30/09/2008. The capped rate detailed is the maximum amount you will pay under this scheme. Payments are calculated on the introductory rate or the standard variable rate, whichever is the lower. Maximum loan to value 75% outside society's local area. Capital repayments up to 10% allowed each year without penalty.

For all interest rates listed please check the current rate with the provider.

Scottish Widows Bank

Rate:	4.09% – two years. Then variable rate (4.74% currently)
Product type:	Discount
Amount of mortgage:	£100,000
Property value:	£150,000
Mortgage type:	Interest only
Total cost (for one year):	£4,090

Monthly Costs

Initial monthly payment:	£340.83
Monthly payment at lender's standard variable rate:	£395.00

Set-up Costs

Mortgage indemnity premium:	N/A
Arrangement fee:	Nil
Less cash-back:	Nil
Net costs:	Nil
Other incentives:	Valuation fees refunded – max £250
	Legal fees refunded – max £150

Conditions

Early redemption penalty:	Legal and valuation fees reclaimed within three years.
Conditional insurances:	None
How much you can borrow:	Single income: 5 times
	Joint incomes: 5 times main income plus 1 times second income or 4 × joint income.

Additional Features

Will not lend in Northern Ireland. 0.65% discount. Offset mortgage facility, mortgage deposit account must be opened in same name(s) as mortgage account. Available only to medical doctors, dentists, solicitors, accountants, vets, teachers. (Must be fully qualified and practising.) Lender charges interest on a daily basis. Payment holidays allowed. Professional mortgage: lending available up to 110% LTV, additional 10% is on unsecured basis over a maximum ten-year period. Valuation fee refunded on completion.

Halifax

Rate:	5.19% – 30/11/2013. Then variable rate (5.5% currently)
Product type:	Fixed
Amount of mortgage:	£100,000
Property value:	£150,000
Mortgage type:	Interest only
Total cost (for one year):	£5,389

Monthly Costs

Initial monthly payment:	£432.50
Monthly payment at lender's standard variable rate:	£458.33

Set-up Costs

Mortgage indemnity premium:	N/A
Arrangement fee:	£199
Less cash-back:	Nil
Net costs:	£199
Other incentives:	None

Conditions

Early redemption penalty:	5% until 30/11/2009 then 4%, 3%, 2% and 1% until 30/11/2013.
Conditional insurances:	None
How much you can borrow:	Single income: 4.53 times Joint incomes: 4.53 times main income plus 1 times second income or 3.4 × joint income.

Additional Features

Lender charges interest on a daily basis. Capital repayments up to 10% allowed each year without penalty. Ability to overpay and underpay.

Abbey National and Coventry building societies also offer greater than four times. Please contact them independently.

Guarantor Mortgages

Here are all the guarantor mortgage providers.

Newcastle Building Society
Tel: 0191 244 2000

Rate and term   Initial rate – 5.99% fixed (5.7% APR) for four years.
After four years – the prevailing standard variable mortgage base rate for the remainder of the term.

Loan amount   £60,000–£500,000

Incentives   10% of loan can be repaid penalty free each year.

Early repayment charges   If you repay your mortgage on or before the four-year period an early repayment charge will apply. The charge will be 5% of your current balance outstanding. Payments less then £500 and/or your monthly payments do not qualify as capital repayments.

Leeds and Holbeck Building Society
Tel: 08450 50 50 62

Rate and term	5.5% APR up to 95% loan to value
Loan amount	£15,000–£250,000
Incentives	10% of loan can be repaid penalty free each year.
Early repayment charges	Early repayment fee of 6/5/4 months interest at standard variable rate.

Yorkshire Building Society offers a guarantor facility across all their mortgage products. You can contact them on 0845 1200 805.

Self-Certification Mortgages

Here are the best no-proof of income lenders.

Name	Rate	Max %	Fee	Cash-back	Redemption	Notes
Coventry	4.48% discount until 31/08/2006	85%	£295	Nil	six months until 31/08/2006	scheme will qualify for privilege rate (currently 5.28%) on 01/01/2009
Northern Rock	4.69% fixed until 01/10/2005	85%	£495	£700 remortgage, £500 purchase	2% of original loan on full redemption until 01/10/2005. Repay cash-back within three years in full	lender charges interest on a daily basis
Scottish Widows Bank	4.89% fixed until 31/10/2008	90%	£295	Nil	3% of amount until 31/10/2008 plus any benefits reclaimed within three years	flexible product
Irish Permanent	4.49% two year discount tracker	90%	£350	Nil	5% within two years	capital repayments upto 20% allowed each year without penalty
Bristol and West	5.45% fixed 30/09/2006	90%	£299	Nil	5% until 30/09/2006 plus administration fee £100	only self-employed applicants who have been trading for one year

Unsecured Loan Providers

There are, again, loads of unsecured loan providers. I've chosen all the sub-7% interest rate lenders offering the best value.

Lombard Direct

Rate:	6.6%
Amount:	£10,000
Term:	five years
Monthly repayment:	£195.23
Total repayable:	£11,713.80
Max term:	seven years
Early repayment penalties:	two months
Additional features:	on-line decision

Notes: Internet applications only. Lombard Direct Personal Loan APRs shown are typical rates, exact cost will depend on personal circumstances and credit assessment. Must be aged between 22 and 65 years old. On-line decision is available.

AA

Rate:	6.6%
Amount:	£10,000
Term:	five years
Monthly repayment:	£195.23
Total repayable:	£11,713.80
Max term:	seven years
Early repayment penalties:	two months
Additional features:	immediate on-line decision

Notes: Available to anyone aged between 18 and 65 with a regular income. Loans available from £1,000 to £25,000. Rates fixed for the term of the loan. Repayments by direct debit only. Cheque could be delivered within 24 hours of successful application. Different rates may be offered depending on personal circumstances, credit assessment procedure and other related factors.

Northern Rock plc

Rate: 6.7%

Amount: £10,000

Term: five years

Monthly Repayment: £195.67

Total Repayable: £11,740.20

Max Term: five years

Early Repayment Penalties: none

Notes: Applicants must be aged between 21 and 80. Loans are subject to credit checks, credit scoring, references, the loan application meeting Northern Rock's personal loans lending policy and that applicants are not unemployed. Rates fixed for term and are typical over a three-year term Typical rate up to three years is 9.9%. Rate is dependent on term and amount, please refer to lender.

Marks and Spencer

Rate: 6.7%

Amount: £10,000

Term: five years

Monthly repayment: £195.67

Total repayable: £11,740.20

Max term: five years

Early repayment penalties: two months

Notes: A different rate may be offered depending on personal circumstances, the credit assessment procedure and other related credit, which will be fixed for the term of the loan. A lower monthly cost is available than with a standard loan by deferring up to 60% of the amount borrowed. At the end of the term customers have the option to repay the deferred amount or continue with the same monthly repayments until the balance is cleared.

Tesco Personal Finance

Rate: 6.9%

Amount: £10,000

Term: five years

Monthly repayment: £196.56

Total repayable: £11,793.60

Max term: five years

Early repayment penalties: two months

Additional features: includes 0.5% discount for on-line applications

Notes: Rates shown include a 0.5% discount for internet applications only and are for a 'typical' customer. Exact rate will be quoted on application. Amounts for over £15,000 are available at a slightly lower APR and can be repaid over a maximum of ten years but cannot be used for debt consolidation. Repayment by direct debit only.

Direct Line

Rate:	6.9%
Amount:	£10,000
Term:	five years
Monthly repayment:	£196.56
Total repayable:	£11,793.60
Max term:	five years
Early repayment penalties:	one month
Additional features:	telephone applications only

Notes: Telephone applications only. Rates fixed for term. Rates shown are typical APRs. Available to anyone over 22 years old subject to status. Loan must be paid by direct debit.

First Direct

Rate:	6.9%
Amount:	£10,000
Term:	five years
Monthly repayment:	£196.56
Total repayable:	£11,793.60
Max term:	seven years
Early repayment penalties:	one month

Notes: Applicants must have lender's cheque account. Rates fixed for term. Typical APR of 6.9% applies to preferential rate loans which are offered to the majority of First Direct customers. First Direct standard rate loans have a typical APR of 9.9%.

Abbey National

Rate: 6.9%

Amount: £10,000

Term: five years

Monthly repayment: £196.56

Total repayable: £11,793.60

Max term: eight years

Early repayment penalties: two months

Additional features: internet applications only

Notes: Applications subject to status. Applicants must be over 18 years of age with a regular income and previous financial commitments without any problems. Rates shown apply to on-line applications only. Different rates apply for non-internet applications. No set-up fees or deposit required. Optional payment protection.

Sainsbury's Bank

Rate:	6.9%
Amount:	£10,000
Term:	five years
Monthly repayment:	£196.56
Total repayable:	£11,793.60
Max term:	five years
Early repayment penalties:	two months
Additional features:	internet applications only

Notes: Applicants must be at least 18 and a UK resident (excluding the Channel Islands and the Isle of Man). Deferred start option available.

0% Credit Card Providers

Here are all the companies that will lend you money for free! Be sure to juggle these cards on time as they can sting you if you are not careful.

Card provider:	Halifax plc
Card name:	h2x
APR % for purchase:	9.9%
APR % cash withdrawals:	18.5%
Cash withdrawal fee per cent:	2%
Cash withdrawal minimum fee:	£2
Minimum salary required to apply:	£25,000
Intro rate:	0%
Introductory rate period:	five months
Maximum interest-free period:	59 days
Existing card debt transfer allowed:	✓
Travel/accident insurance:	Up to £100k
Purchase protection:	Up to 100 days
Loyalty bonus/cash-back:	None

Notes: Introductory rate applies to balance transfers for the first five months. Thereafter, the rate increases to 9.9% and applies to purchases and balance transfers. Account can be managed on-line with contact to the provider by email. Paper statements available on request, charged at £3 a time. Phone calls to h2x will be charged at premium rate. Access to the Halifax Shopping Extra site. Free additional card.

Card provider:	Capital One
Card name:	Platinum
APR % for purchase:	10.9%
APR % cash withdrawals:	20.5%
Cash withdrawal fee per cent:	1.5%
Cash withdrawal minimum fee:	£2
Minimum salary required to apply:	£10,000
Intro rate:	0%
Introductory rate period:	six months
Maximum interest-free period:	54 days
Existing card debt transfer allowed:	✓
Travel/accident insurance:	None
Purchase protection:	None
Loyalty bonus/cash-back:	None

Notes: Minimum age 21 years. 0% introductory rate applies to all new purchases for first six months. Balance transfers from other cards pay 4.9% APR fixed until the balance is cleared if transferred within six months of account opening. Optional payment protection insurance. Discounts available on travel, hotels and eating.

Card provider:	Barclaycard
Card name:	Classic
APR % for purchase:	11.9%
APR % cash withdrawals:	19.3%
Cash withdrawal fee per cent:	1.5%
Cash withdrawal minimum fee:	£2
Minimum salary required to apply:	N/A
Intro rate:	0%
Introductory rate period:	until repaid
Maximum interest-free period:	56 days
Existing card debt transfer allowed:	✓
Travel/accident insurance:	up to £50k
Purchase protection:	100 days up to £1,500 per item
Loyalty bonus/cash-back:	rewards

Notes: Visa or Mastercard. Introductory rate applies to balance transfers only and is fixed until the transfer balance is fully repaid. Typical standard APRs shown but these are subject to personal circumstances and therefore a higher rate may apply. Fee waived if £5,000 + per annum spent. No fee on second card. £50 cheque guarantee card. International rescue, legal help and home assistance services available. Customers who transfer a balance and continue to use their card for purchases (at lease £50 a month) will qualify for 0% on the transferred balance until it is paid off. If a customer does not use their card for a month then the transferred balance will be charged at a low rate of 6.9% for that month. If spending re-commences the following month, the rate will drop back to the 0% on the transferred balance. No more than five balance transfers can be made each calendar year. The maximum you can transfer each calendar month is £5,000, subject to total available credit on your account.

Card provider:	LloydsTSB
Card name:	Advance
APR % for purchase:	11.9%
APR % cash withdrawals:	14.2%
Cash withdrawal fee per cent:	1.5%
Cash withdrawal minimum fee:	£1.50
Minimum salary required to apply:	N/A
Intro rate:	0%
Introductory rate period:	six months
Maximum interest-free period:	0 days
Existing card debt transfer allowed:	✓
Travel/accident insurance:	None
Purchase protection:	None
Loyalty bonus/cash-back:	None

Notes: Introductory rate applies to balance transfers and purchases until 01/01/2004. Internet fraud protection. No annual fee. Optional payment protection. Best price cover if buying something new worth up to £1,000 and seeing it cheaper later, card holders could claim back the difference (less the first £25 and excluding goods such as holidays, food, travel, clothing and motor accessories.) Free extended warranty scheme.

Card provider:	First Direct
Card name:	Gold Visa
APR % for purchase:	13.9%
APR % cash withdrawals:	16%
Cash withdrawal fee per cent:	1.75%
Cash withdrawal minimum fee:	£2
Minimum salary required to apply:	N/A
Intro rate:	0%
Introductory rate period:	six months
Maximum interest-free period:	56 days
Existing card debt transfer allowed:	✓
Travel/accident insurance:	up to £50k
Purchase protection:	None
Loyalty bonus/cash-back:	None

Notes: Introductory rate applies for six months for balance transfers over £500. Free personal liability insurance up to £1million. Card free if spending is in excess of £1,200 a year. Transactions can be viewed via First Direct PC Banking with authorisation.

Card provider:	Egg
Card name:	Credit Card
APR % for purchase:	13.9%
APR % cash withdrawals:	16.3%
Cash withdrawal fee per cent:	1.25%
Cash withdrawal minimum fee:	£2
Minimum salary required to apply:	N/A
Intro rate:	0%
Introductory rate period:	six months
Maximum interest-free period:	45 days
Existing card debt transfer allowed:	✓
Travel/accident insurance:	None
Purchase protection:	In transit – 30 days
Loyalty bonus/cash-back:	Cash-back

Notes: Visa card. APRs (variable) are 12.3% (0% fixed until 1 February 2004 for new purchases and balance transfers for new accounts opened between 1 July 2003 and 31 July 2003. 0.5% cash-back on any transaction. Cash-back is paid once a year and maximum amount will be £500. Payments must be made by direct debit or transfer from an egg saving account. Application and card management are on-line only (www.egg.com). Charges will be made if internet facilities are not used where appropriate.

Card provider: Virgin Money

Card name: Card Option A

APR % for purchase: 13.9%

APR % cash withdrawals: 15.7%

Cash withdrawal fee per cent: 1.5%

Cash withdrawal minimum fee: £2

Minimum salary required to apply: N/A

Intro rate: 0%

Introductory rate period: six months

Maximum interest-free period: 59 days

Existing card debt transfer allowed: ✓

Travel/accident insurance: Up to £100k

Purchase protection: First 100 days up to £1,000

Loyalty bonus/cash-back: Access to members' shop

Notes: Mastercard. Minimum age is 18 years. No annual fee. Applications via post, telephone or on-line. Introductory rate applies for first six months. Customers are matched to an option which suits their requirements. Additional benefits include loyalty scheme, choice of card design, up to three free additional cards, 24 hour customer service and members' shop service.

Card provider:	Nationwide BS
Card name:	Classic
APR % for purchase:	13.9%
APR % cash withdrawals:	11.9%
Cash withdrawal fee per cent:	1%
Cash withdrawal minimum fee:	£1
Minimum salary required to apply:	N/A
Intro rate:	0%
Introductory rate period:	six months
Maximum interest-free period:	56 days
Existing card debt transfer allowed:	✓
Travel/accident insurance:	up to £50k
Purchase protection:	100 days for certain items above £50
Loyalty bonus/cash-back:	none

Notes: Available to those aged 18 or over and resident in the UK subject to status. Introductory rates apply to purchases and balance transfers for the first six months after issue.

For all interest rates listed please check the current rate with the provider.

Credit Reference Agencies

There are two credit reference agencies – Experian and Equifax. If you require a copy of your credit file send them:

- £2 fee
- full name
- date of birth
- residential addresses for the last six years.

Their addresses are:

Experian Consumer Help Service, PO Box 8000, Nottingham NG1 5GX

Equifax Credit File Advice Centre, PO Box 3001, Glasgow G81 2DT

Auction Houses

Here is a list of all the auction houses that regularly hold auctions selling properties. You have to request a catalogue and register to attend. In most cases this is for free.

Allsop and Co, 100 Knightsbridge, London SW1X 7LB. Tel: (020) 7494 3686

Andrews and Robertson, 27 Camberwell Green, London SE5 7AN. Tel: 020 7703 2662

Athawes Son and Co, The Auctioneers Offices, 203 High St, London W3. Tel: (020) 8992 0056

Barnard Marcus, Commercial House, 64–66 Glenthorne Road, London W6 0LR. Tel: (0336) 424572

Countrywide Property Auctions, 144 New London Road, Chelmsford, Essex CM2 0AW. Tel: (01245) 344133

Drivers and Norris, 407 Holloway Road, London N7 6HP. Tel: (020) 7607 5001

Edwin Evans, 253 Lavender Hill, London SW11 1JW. Tel: (020) 7228 5864

FPD Savills London, 139 Sloane Street, London SW1X 9AY. Tel: (020) 7824 9091

FPD Savills Nottingham, 4 St Peters Gate, Nottingham NG1 2JG. Tel: (0115) 934 8000

Halifax Property Services. Tel: (01509) 680701

Harman Healy, 340 Grays Inn Road, London WC1X 8BJ. Tel: (020) 7833 5885

Keith Pattinson. Tel: 0800 649234

McHugh and Co, 71 Parkway, Regents Park, London NW1 7PP. Tel: (020) 7485 0112

Nelson Bakewell, Westland House, 17c Curzon Street, London W1Y 8LT. Tel: (020) 7626 6501

Pugh and Company, 11 Cross Street, Preston PR1 3LT. Tel: (01772) 883399

Strettons, Central House, 189–203 Hoe Street, London E17 3AP. Tel: (020) 8520 8383

Ward and Partners, 136 Ashford Road, Bearsted, Maidstone, Kent ME14 4NH. Tel: (01622) 736736

William H Brown Spalding, 18–19 Sheep Market, Spalding, Lincs PE11 1BG. Tel: (01775) 711711

Winkworth and Co, 23 Brighton Road, South Croydon CR2 6EA. Tel: (020) 8649 7255

Affordable Areas

All these areas are affordable because there are properties on the market now that are less than four times the average salary for that area. Get hunting!

East Anglia

Attleborough, Norfolk
Boston, Lincs
Brookenby, Lincs
Bungay, Norfolk
Chatteris, Cambs
Cromer, Norfolk
Downham Market, Norfolk
Eye, Suffolk
Grantham, Lincs
Hadleigh, Suffolk
Ipswich, Suffolk
Kings Lynn, Norfolk
Lincoln, Lincs
Market Rasen, Lincs
Mundesley, Norfolk
Norwich, Norfolk
Orton Goldhay, Peterborough
Orton Malbourne, Peterborough
St Neots, Cambs
Skegness, Lincs
Sudbury, Suffolk
Welland, Peterborough
Wickham Market, Woodbridge,
  Suffolk
Wisbech, Cambs

Midlands

Anstey Heights, Leicester
Aspley, Notts
Bedford, Bedfordshire
Bestwood, Notts
Bilborough, Notts
Binley, Coventry
Bobbersmill, Notts
Braunstone, Leicester
Broxtowe, Notts
Bulwell, Notts
Burton-on-Trent, Staffs
Camphill, Coventry
Clifton, Notts
Corby, Northants
Daventry, Warwickshire
Dunstable, Bedfordshire
Foleshill, Coventry
Highbury Vale, Notts
Hodge Hill, Birmingham
Ilkeston, Notts
Irthlingborough, Northants
Kettering, Northants
Kimberley, Notts
Kirkby-in-Ashfield, Notts
Leicester City Centre, Leicester

Luton, Bedfordshire
Mansfield, Notts
Moulton, Northants
Newark, Notts
Newcastle-under-Lyme, Staffs
Newstead Village, Hucknall, Notts
Northampton, Northants
Oldbury, West Midlands
Rednal, Birmingham
Rugby, Warwickshire
Rushden, Northants
Shrewsbury
Stoke-on-Trent, Staffs
Strelley, Notts
Sutton-in-Ashfield, Notts
The Meadows, Notts
Thorncywood, Notts
Thorpelands, Northants
Top Valley, Notts
Walsall, West Midlands
Warren Hill, Notts
Wellingborough, Northants
Willenhall, Coventry
Wolverhampton, West Midlands

North

Accrington
Allerton, Liverpool
Bacup, Manchester
Balby, Doncaster
Barnsley, Lancs
Beeston, Leeds
Birkenhead, Lancs
Blackburn
Blackpool
Bolton
Bootle, Liverpool
Bradford
Broughton, Cheshire
Bury, Lancs

Castleford
Chester, Cheshire
Clayton, Manchester
Colne, Lancs
Crewe, Cheshire
Crossgates, Leeds
Darwen, Lancs
Denton, Manchester
Derby
Dewsbury
Dudley
Eccles, Manchester
Eddington, Doncaster
Farnworth, Lancs
Gainsborough, Manchester
Garforth
Golborne, Cheshire
Goole
Grimsby, Yorkshire
Halifax
Holywell, Flintshire
Huddersfield, Yorkshire
Hull
Huyton, Prescot
Hyde Park, Manchester
Keighley
Kirkby, Maghull
Leigh, Lancs
Liverpool L4
Liverpool L6
Liverpool L7
Liverpool L8
Liverpool L9
Liverpool L13
Liverpool L14
Liverpool L20
Longsight, Manchester
Marsden, Yorkshire
Mexborough
Morecombe, Lancs

Moss Side, Manchester
Northwich, Cheshire
Openshaw, Manchester
Peasley Cross, Merseyside
Pocklington, Yorkshire
Preston
Rishton, Lancs
Rock Ferry, Bebington
Rochdale, Lancs
Rotherham
Roundhay
Runcorn, Cheshire
Rusholme, Manchester
St Helens, Merseyside
Salford, Manchester
Scarborough, Yorkshire
Scunthorpe
Sheffield City Centre
Skipton, Bradford
Swinton, Manchester
Wakefield, Yorkshire
Wallasey
Walton Vale, Lancs
Warrington, Lancs
Waterloo, Lancs
West Derby
Wigan
Winsford, Cheshire
Withlington, Manchester
Wombwell
Worksop, Manchester
Worsley, Manchester

North East England

Arthurs Hill, Newcastle
Benwell, Newcastle
Bishops Auckland, Darlington
Blakelaw, West Denton
Blyth, Newcastle
Carlisle, Northumberland

Chilton, Darlington
Colliery, Durham
Consett
Elswick, Tyne & Wear
Ferryhill, Spennymoor
Gateshead, Newcastle
Hartlepool
Hebburn
Hendon, Sunderland
Hexham, Northumberland
Houghton-le-Spring
Lemington, West Denton
Middlesbrough, Cleveland
Newcastle-upon-Tyne, Northumberland
Newton Aycliffe, Darlington
Prudhoe, Northumberland
Redcar, Cleveland
Ryton, Crawcrook
Seaham
South Shields, Newcastle
Stockton-on-Tees, Cleveland
Walkergate, Tyne and Wear
Wallsend, Newcastle
Washington, Tyne & Wear

South England

Bexhill-on-sea, Sussex
Bognor Regis, Portsmouth
Bournemouth, Dorset
Fareham, Hampshire
Rottingdean, Brighton
Rowner, Gosport
Ryde, Isle Of Wight
St Leonards-on-sea, East Sussex
St Marys, Southampton
Sandown, Isle Of Wight
Shirley, Southampton
Sholing, Southampton
Southbourne, Dorset

Southsea, Hampshire
Thornhill, Southampton

South East England
Ashford, Kent
Broadstairs, Kent
Canterbury, Kent
Chatham, Kent
Cliftonville, Kent
Dartford, Kent
Dover, Kent
Eastbourne, Sussex
Erith, Kent
Faversham, Kent
Folkstone, Kent
Hastings, East Sussex
Herne Bay, Kent
Margate, Kent
Ramsgate, Kent
Rochester, Kent
Sittingbourne, Kent
Snodland, Kent
Westgate-on-sea, Kent

South West England
Avon, Bristol
Axminster, Devon
Bodmin, Cornwall
Bovey Tracey, Devon
Bridgewater, Taunton
Callington, Cornwall
Chard, Somerset
Chelston, Torquay, Devon
Clevedon, Bristol
Dawlish, Devon
Devonport, Plymouth
Filton, Bristol
Gillingham, Dorset
Honicknowle, Plymouth

Hooe, Plymouth
Houndstone, Somerset
Ilfracombe, Devon
Ilminster, Somerset
Keyham, Plymouth
Laira, Plymouth
Launceston, Cornwall
Lipson, Plymouth
Looe, Plymouth
Paignton, Devon
Plymouth City Centre, Plymouth
St Budeaux, Plymouth
Shepton Mallet, Somerset
Stoke, Plymouth
Stratton Creber, Newquay
Tavistock, Devon
Teignmouth, Devon
Topsham, Devon
Torquay, Devon
Wellington, Somerset
Westbury, Bath
Weston Super Mare, Somerset
Yeovil, Somerset

West England
Caldicot, Gloucs
Churchdown, Gloucs
Cinderford, Gloucs
Coleford, Gloucs
Hardwicke, Gloucs
Hereford, Herefordshire
Kidderminster, Worcs
Newtown Farm, Herefordshire
Redditch, Worcs
Tewkesbury, Gloucs
Worcester, Worcs

Essex, Hertfordshire and Middlesex
Aveley, Essex
Basildon, Essex
Clacton-on-sea, Essex
Colchester, Essex
Dagenham, Essex
East Tilbury, Essex
Enfield, Essex
Frinton-on-sea, Essex
Grays, Essex
Halstead, Essex
Harlow, Essex
Harold Hill, Essex
Harwich, Essex
Hornchurch, Essex
Laindon, Essex
Pitsea, Essex
Purfleet, Essex
Rainham, Essex
Romford, Essex
Sawbridgeworth, Herts
Sheerness, Essex
Shoeburyness, Essex
South Ockendon, Essex
Southend, Essex
Stanford le Hope, Essex
Tilbury, Essex
Waltham Cross, Essex
Westcliffe-on-sea, Essex
Wickford, Essex
Witham, Essex

London
Beckton
Bexley Heath
Leyton
Northolt
Plaistow

Streatham
Thamesmead
Walthamstow
West Hendon
Woolwich

Scotland
Airdrie, Lanarkshire
Alexandria, Dumbarton
Beith, Bridge of Weir
Bellshill
Bridgeton, Glasgow
Broxburn, Livingston
Carstairs Junction, Lanarkshire
Chapelhall, Airdrie
Cleland, Lanarkshire
Craigshill, Livingston
Cronberry, Ayr
Dalry, Bridge of Weir
Darvel, Kilmarnock
Dennistown, Glasgow
Dumbarton, Dumbartonshire
East Kilbride, Glasgow
Falkirk
Glengarnock, Bridge of Weir
Glenrothes
Greenock, Refrewshire
Govanhill, Glasgow
Hamilton
Ibrox, Glasgow
Inverheithing, Dalgety Bay
Kilbirnie, Bridge of Weir
Kilsyth, Glasgow
Kilwinning, Troon
Kirkcaldy
Kirkintolloch, Bishopbriggs
Lochgelly, Dumfermline
Maybole, Ayr
New Cumnock, Ayr
Newmilus, Kilmarnock, Ayrshire

North Carbrain, Cumberland
Paisley
Port Glasgow, Refrewshire
Priesthill, Glasgow
Saracen Cross, Glasgow
Springboig, Glasgow
Stewarton, Kilmarnock
Tollcross, Glasgow
Whitburn, Livingston
Wishaw, Lanarkshire
Yoker, Glasgow

Wales

Abercynon, Pontypridd
Abertillery, Ebbw Vale
Caerphilly
Church Village, Pontypridd
Edwardsville, Pontypridd
Ely, Rhiwbina
Gilfach Goch, Pontypridd
Greenfield Terrace, Ebbw Vale
Neath, Glamorgan
Port Talbot, Glamorgan
Treharris, Pontypridd

Mortgage/Loan and Credit Card Providers

Mortgage Providers

Alliance and Leicester, 113
Bank of Ireland, 108, 113
Bank of Scotland Mortgage Direct, 85, 101
Beverley BS, 115
Birmingham Midshires, 89
BM Solutions, 106
Bristol and West, 96, 106, 109, 121
Britannic Money plc, 98
Capital Home Loans, 88
Chelsea, 106, 113
Coventry, 121
Direct Line Mortgages, 80
Halifax, 117
Home Loans Direct, 92
Irish Permanent, 87, 121
Kensington Mortgage Co, 91, 106
Kent Reliance BS, 105
Leeds and Holbeck Building Society, 120
Leek United, 103
Mortgage Express, 100
Nat West, 82
Newcastle Building Society, 119
Northern Rock, 77, 93, 111, 113, 121
Principality, 113
Royal Bank of Scotland, 81
Sainsbury's Bank, 83
Scarborough, 90, 113
Scottish Widows Bank, 78, 102, 116, 121

Staffordshire BS, 110
Stroud and Swindon, 104
Sun Bank, 99
UCB Home Loans, 97
West Bromwich, 95, 113
Yorkshire BS, 76

Loan Providers

AA, 124
Abbey National, 130
Direct Line, 128
First Direct, 129
Lombard Direct, 123
Marks and Spencer, 126
Northern Rock plc, 125
Sainsbury's Bank, 131
Tesco Personal Finance, 127

Credit Card Providers

Barclaycard, 135
Capital One, 134
Egg, 138
First Direct, 137
Halifax plc, 133
Lloyds TSB, 136
Nationwide BS, 140
Virgin Money, 139

Index

Other Services

The author also offers a portfolio building service to clients of all sizes. He will help with:

- Sourcing the right properties tailored to your own strategy.
- Raising the cheapest finance to purchase the properties.
- Finding the right tenants.
- The ongoing maintenance of the properties.

If you are thinking of building a portfolio or need help expanding your portfolio then contact:

Ajay Ahuja BSc ACA
Accountants Direct
99 Moreton Road
Ongar
Essex
CM5 0AR

Tel: 0800 652 3979
Fax: 01277 362563
Email: emergencyaccountants@yahoo.co.uk
Web: www.buytolethotspots.com